"Jack Hayford locates effectual prayer at the center of Kingdom living, which is also in the midst of the cosmic battle between good and evil. Everyone lives in it, whether they know it or not, and most of what really happens between us and the texture of our lives with those closest to us. To be able to work with God in prayer for the good of those we love is a great gift of grace, but we must act with understanding to secure it. Pastor Hayford places the human heart under the microscope of Scripture to reveal the inner dynamics of a life that pulls those closest to us into the loving sway of God's actions.

What Pastor Hayford leads us into is healthy, strong, effectual and theologically deep. If you would like to see dear ones moved toward God, he tells you how. If a wide range of self-identified Christians studied and followed this book, the churches and the moral and spiritual climate of our world would change radically. My best advice is to read it and put it into practice."

—**Dallas Willard**, bestselling author, *The Divine Conspiracy*; professor of philosophy, University of Southern California

"As everyone familiar with the wonderful writings of Jack Hayford would expect, this book is rich with all we need to understand how to intercede powerfully for the people we care about most. It is rich in Scripture-based teaching, personal experience, practical advice and helpful instruction. Jack Hayford was my pastor for 23 years and taught me nearly everything I know about prayer, yet this book has newly inspired me to pray. I am hopeful and joyfully expectant on a deeper level than ever as I await the answers to these prayers. Everyone wanting to learn how to maximize their prayer impact should know that this book is a gift for them and they would do well to open it."

—**Stormie Omartian**, bestselling author, *The Power of a Praying Wife*, *The Power of a Praying Husband*, *The Power of a Praying Woman* and many others

"For more than thirty years, Pastor Jack Hayford has been a valued, respected voice to the Body of Christ—especially in the areas of worship, life in the Spirit and prayer. In the days we are living in, I can't think of anything more important than the subject of this book—praying for those you love. Pastor Jack's profound yet practical insights into this subject will fill you with hope and move you into a passionate pursuit of praying for the people you love! I urge you to read this book."

—**Michael W. Smith**, singer/songwriter

"Jack Hayford has been one of my most important spiritual mentors for many years. His spiritual intimacy with Christ, personal integrity and biblical knowledge make him a trusted guide and beloved pastor. This book, *Praying for Those You Love*, is powerful and insightful. It not only has the ability to change your life, but it can change the legacy of your family for generations."

—**Jimmy Evans**, founder and president, MarriageToday

"For more than 25 years, Jack Hayford has been my pastor, spiritual father and teacher of all things God. One of the many qualities he exudes brilliantly is balance. *Praying for Those You Love* is one more wonderful example. I was freshly reminded that God entrusts us to plant the seeds, and then we entrust Him to bring the harvest. We are called to fight and we are instructed to rest. There is a time to let go yet persevere in prayer. This book is a practical and encouraging teaching on the privilege of partnering with God—heaven on earth."

—**Lisa Whelchel**, bestselling author, *Creative Correction* and *The Facts of Life and Other Lessons My Father Taught Me*

"Pastor Jack Hayford has done it again! *Praying for Those You Love* captivated me from the first word. I was stirred, convicted and inspired by the Holy Spirit in an area in which I need and want to go deeper. As a pastor, I knew immediately that my life and the church where I pastor would never be the same. This book is a must-read for every believer and church leader. Your life and the lives of those you love will forever be changed!"

—**Pastor Robert Morris**, senior pastor, Gateway Church, Southlake, Texas; bestselling author, *The Blessed Life*

THE
SECRETS OF
INTERCESSORY
PRAYER

JACK HAYFORD

Chosen

a division of Baker Publishing Group
Minneapolis, Minnesota

Previously published under the title *Praying for Those You Love*

Published by Chosen Books
11400 Hampshire Avenue South
Bloomington, Minnesota 55438
www.chosenbooks.com

Chosen Books is a division of
Baker Publishing Group, Grand Rapids, Michigan

Printed in the United States of America

Library of Congress Cataloging-in-Publication Data is available for this title.

ISBN 978-0-8007-9545-0

Cover design by Kirk DouPonce, DogEared Design

Contents

FOREWORD

Our God is one of relationship. He is passionate about our relationship with Him and our relationships with each other. It's how we are wired and designed, each one made in the image of our Creator—to nurture, love and care for others both in our immediate sphere and beyond. Psalm 133 says that where there is unity, God commands a blessing, so it should be of no surprise that the area where there is most potential for *much* blessing across the earth is also the area facing insidious attack and catastrophic breakdown, which, in turn, has affected every sphere of our society.

Pastor Jack has poured his heart, wisdom and experience into these pages, as he explores the reason for such tension within relationships and instructs us on how to pray effectively, with all we are, over those we love and those in our sphere of influence, whatever the past has looked like. The power of God's redemptive plan for us covers every experience that has brought much heartache—that His plan includes restoration and a new beginning.

I know in my own life, and I am sure in yours, the most painful experiences have been where relationship has been fractured or where misunderstandings have caused such deep distress that wading your way back to strength in these matters may have seemed much easier to put in the impossible category. But it is *right here*, in the seemingly unbearable, that our God *still* reigns. He is the God of the impossible, for when we are weak, He is strong and ever faithful to reside over the promise of His Word.

> Be cheerful no matter what; pray all the time; thank God no matter what happens. This is the way God wants you who belong to Christ Jesus to live.
>
> 1 Thessalonians 5:16–18, THE MESSAGE

I know your heart will be stirred to action as you read, and I for one am ever grateful for the life of our dear friend Pastor Jack as he once again leads the way.

Much love always,
Darlene Zschech

1

A Divine Invitation to Partnership

Then He taught them many things by parables, and said to them in His teaching: "Listen! Behold, a sower went out to sow. And it happened, as he sowed, that some seed fell by the wayside; and the birds of the air came and devoured it. . . . And some seed fell among thorns; and the thorns grew up and choked it, and it yielded no crop. But other seed fell on good ground and yielded a crop that sprang up, increased and produced."

Mark 4:2–4, 7–8

Whether you are married, a parent, a relative, a pastor of a congregation or simply a person with good friends who are close enough to you to be "dear," to be loved, let me begin by asking you two questions:

- Are you aware that the living, loving God who made you, each of them and me, loves them too, and at a depth of love neither you nor I can fathom?
- Would you feel profited to discover principles of partnership with Him, whereby your prayers for their well-being—especially if they are either indifferent, distant or even opposed to a relationship—would become focused with spiritual clarity and faith in His Word, thereby becoming more than guesswork?

My guess is that your answer has been yes to those inquiries even before I asked them here. Most people's are, because most people not only have "loved ones" of family or social relationship, but also believe God is not only real, He is love. And He is.

Now, without seeming to have framed a book of questions rather than answers, or at least help, please let me ask one more. I qualify for all five types of people named in the opening sentence of this book. As a husband, a parent, a friend or relative of many, I have often been troubled by the difficulties of loved ones, including those who have chosen to omit God from their lives. Naturally, that last issue holds ultimate concern for me, but I am never dispassionate about other issues, however temporal. As a pastor, however, there is a distinct—a twofold—burden of privileged responsibility I have borne for the more than forty years of my ministry. I not only need faith and fidelity to live a life of prayer for my flock, I also need wisdom and insight into God's Word to enable me to teach others how to pray effectively with confidence, emboldened, with human and holy discernment and with the Holy Spirit's power.

All that said, here is the third question: Even if you are not a church leader as I am called to be, what would you do if God stepped into your study and spoke these words to you?

Tell the people this: My people, as you look around and you see marriages dissolving in one home after another; as you see young people drifting into increasingly destructive practices; as you note the declining commitment of those around you who are drifting from the moorings of honoring God's Person, Word and ways—understand: This is not more cultural happenstance. It is a blitzkrieg from the darkness—a frontal attack of calculated and evil dimensions plotted by the adversary of God, man and all that is good, and being advanced by cunning, demonic hordes who can only be blocked in one way: prayer.

Call the people to pray. Teach them to counterattack. Unveil My Word to them so that, by calling on Me through the grace I readily give when they invoke the name of My Son, they may unleash My power. As they accept this partnership I call them to, praying that My Kingdom may enter the world of those they love "on earth," I will answer them by My Spirit's power—working My will "as it is in heaven."

Well, that is really what happened. I don't mean, of course, that God stepped into my office in the sense of physical appearance. Rather He made His presence and will known by the means He has revealed in His eternal Word of truth—the Holy Bible. In that book, which is the ultimate authority on all life's issues, both eternal and temporal, He says that He will speak at times to people by "prophecy." In this use, *prophecy* is not a reference to anything arbitrary or arcane—God is never random; nor is He weird. (Toss out the pundits who publish cleverly cast guesswork or the goofs who claim to be plumbing "inner wisdom within us all.")

Thus I took seriously what was spoken to me—not because I think I am smarter than others, but because I am sure God is. And His Word says He will give the gift of such revelations to awaken us to issues we need to deal with—personally, as a group or congregation or as a nation. We must be consummately clear that such prophecies, for example, the "word" I received that day, are infinitely less in authority than the Bible—His unchanging written Word. When He breathes these prophecies into our understanding, He expects us to measure what we hear and be guided in our response by the principles established in Scripture.

This book, then, is among the responses that seek to address the means by which people like us can confront the blitzkrieg—the wave of forces that seek to destroy the well-being, homes, families and marriages of ones we love, and drag many dear souls we care about down a pathway of eternal loss.

It is time for you and me to awaken—but not to a frenzy of fear. With passion rooted in understanding we can learn to pray for God's intervening goodness in the lives of those we love. The prayers will vary—a child may be wandering from God; a best friend may need strength for a difficult task; a marital relationship may be strained; a fellow laborer in ministry may need healing or guidance or mercy. Regardless of the cries of our hearts, the fact that we are living in a crisis of human and spiritual need means it is an opportune moment for the entry of God's grace, goodness and power.

That is why I can smile as I write, though I feel the issue at hand is critical, and why I can sleep at night, though dear ones are deep in problems that I do not take lightly. I want you to approach this book as a source of great encouragement, not only to engage earnest prayer for God's intervention, but also to pray with clear-headed faith and practical wisdom that lay hold of the power of partnership with almighty God.

God's will that the affairs of humankind be managed via partnership with Him goes back to the beginning. He has indicated His desire to release His power *in our world* when we request it *from His throne.* It is the truth at the core of the best known prayer in the world, taught to us by His Son, Jesus the Christ, who said, "Pray this way: Our Father, who art in heaven, holy is Your name." Then He gave the "partnership phrase" as a key: "Your Kingdom come, Your will be done *on earth as it is in heaven.*"

I have pondered at length in other writings of mine the depth and dimension of that prayer, and the duties as well as privileges incumbent upon us as we respond to its instructive content. But the one phrase I will focus on as you open these pages with me is the partnership phrase. In short, God has said, "What you ask Me to do as we partner on earth, I'll answer with My love, My power, My wisdom and in My time with all the force of heaven's throne engaging whom and what you ask Me to engage."

Praying "for those you love" is obviously an arena into which God wants us to welcome His power and works. In the midst of unparalleled challenges to our families, along

13

with the severe problems and confused circumstances of others we love, we have an incomparable opportunity to answer it all by taking action in prayer in ways we may have never understood.

The Bible often uses agricultural terms to express God's ways, and He addresses the blessing (or the curse) of a harvest with clarity: He wants to bring people into a harvest of blessing! But He has placed the seed in our hands, giving us promises, saying, "Ask, and it will be given to you; seek, and you will find; knock, and it will be opened to you" (Matthew 7:7) It is as clear as it can be. God is saying, "You take your role in our earth-side setting, and I will answer with My works and wisdom from my heaven-side throne."

Jesus relayed this truth in a similar way, describing a farmer who went out to sow seeds. He told how some seeds fell off to the side, and birds swooped in and devoured them. Interpreting the metaphor He asserted, "The sower sows the Word and there are some who hear it. But then, like birds of the air, Satan comes and snatches away the Word that was sown in their hearts, thwarting the good things God wants to do" (see Mark 4:3–4, 14–15).

Jesus also said in this parable that sometimes seeds take root and hold the promise of a harvest, but then they are overtaken by thorns and yield no crop. He told His followers that this refers to the enemy coming into the midst of good seeds and sowing that which is diminishing and destructive. Jesus labeled them "tares" or "weeds," sown by an intruder to choke out God's intended best. These distractions and deceptions take from people—people like those we love—everything God has benevolently willed for their lives.

When the Savior identified the intruder as Satan (see Mark 4:15), He meant to open our eyes to the fact that life issues, including praying, are not mystical, but they do require our perceiving ongoing spiritual conflict in the invisible realm. Prayer in all regards takes a new frame of reference when we understand the war between God's Kingdom and Satan's dark hordes. This battle, insofar as it involves earth, is one in which God has called us to engage, enlisting us as "knee-soldiers" whose prayer-call for the "incoming" of God's Kingdom will welcome a barrage of God's power to break through the darkness and bring deliverance to people we know.

So join me in "seeing the invisible," the non-mystical reality God's Word reveals. Let us recall the apostle Paul's words: "Brothers, we are not wrestling against flesh and blood, but against principalities and powers, against the rulers of the darkness of this world, against hosts of evil spirits in the invisible realm" (see Ephesians 6:12). And recognizing that God has called us to "sow" unto a holy harvest, know that it will not be realized without a battle. The adversary is a formidable foe, but we need not fear. We take our stance in prayer before God's throne, and He is unimpeachable. Further, He has given His Holy Spirit to fill and empower us, and "greater is he that is in you, than he that is in the world" (1 John 4:4, KJV).

True, the enemy is hard at work. But I want us to see, in contrast to evil snatchings and tares of confusion and disruption in our midst, that you and I hold an important place in helping to bring the Lord's harvest to fruition: There is another outcome for seeds that God sows. See it as you revisit the promise of Psalm 126:6—an "*all seasons*" promise: Those who go forth weeping, bearing precious seed, shall come again at the time of harvest with joy, bringing their sheaves with them.

I call this an "all seasons" promise because it notes how sowing in prayer is often attended by weeping—tears that sometimes reflect the pain our hearts feel over the needs of those we love. I want to urge you to join me in the possibility of tears born in prayer for another reason: passion . . . and eventual *joy*. Prayer that wars against the darkness by stepping before the eternal throne of God's glorious light and presence will never remain dispassionate. And further, as we do so—as we plant His heaven-given promises in the soil of earth's human brokenness, confusion and need—the passion of faith will burst into joyous confidence that God's will *will prevail!*

If hell is pulling out all the stops against marriages, homes and families—against spouses, children and others we love—heaven is ready to answer with victory. The one requirement? Answer God's loving call . . . just as I have since He "stopped by my office" that day, charging me to *Call the people to pray. Teach them to counterattack. Unveil My Word to them so that, by calling on Me through the grace I readily give when they invoke the name of My Son, they may unleash My power. As they accept this partnership I call them to, praying that My Kingdom may enter the world of those they love "on earth," I will answer them by My Spirit's power—working My will "as it is in heaven."*

Let's prepare ourselves and pray. In the next chapter, we will review briefly the battle's beginning, see why the need is so great that we stay rooted in faith-filled prayer, and learn how God made a way for us to come to Him and conquer through Him.

2

The Original Splintering

So when the woman saw that the tree was good for food, that it was pleasant to the eyes, and a tree desirable to make one wise, she took of its fruit and ate. She also gave to her husband with her, and he ate. Then the eyes of both of them were opened.

Genesis 3:6–7

It is the beginning of every problem we face today, and the best place to begin discovering how to pray for those we love: the Fall of man.

Those four words have been commonly understood in Western civilization for at least the five centuries preceding ours. They did not require explanation (and you may not need one either). But the slide of general knowledge (in general!) and the rise of relativism's proposal that "there are absolutely no absolutes" has caused the word *sin* to be freighted no longer with severe implications. Thus the question "When did sin enter the human situation?" is seldom asked.

"Original sin" is another name for the same event, "the Fall of man"—an important reference when we come to the one Book that reaches to us to help us understand "how we humans got this way, and what we can do about it." "This way" is *splintered*; we are at war with ourselves, angry with people we once enjoyed, oft-confused at things in general, seldom keeping focus on things earlier thought important, and so forth. Most of all, that *splintering* brought humankind's separation from the life-source who would have kept everything connected, fulfilling and functional: *God*.

Original sin brought about the Fall of man, and while everything felt the impact, the foremost thing has been *relationships*. Let's make a summary of the effects of the Fall to see how it influenced us as well as those we love. It will help us pray.

The Genesis of Relationships—Good and Bad

In one of the earliest chapters of the Bible every human being is secure in relationship with God. Before we read very far, however, every human being is separated from God. This third chapter of Genesis, the story of Adam and Eve in the Garden and their fall into sin, tells us why it happened, and, further, why families crumble and why any individual outside of Christ is lost.

In His love and mercy, God is quick to set in motion the program of salvation, and He makes a way of reconciliation for the fallen pair, but a problem still exists. The seed of sin has entered the human race, and that spiritually active seed, certainly just as real as a biologically active sperm, was (and is) transmitted to their children. The seed of sin splintered the lifeline between God and humankind, but "amazing grace" was introduced to make restoration possible—with all the relational benefits it can hold, from knowing God and being empowered by His Spirit to live in and enjoy His intended ways for our well-being to relating to one another and growing in marriages, families and communities where people *truly* care and personal insensitivity or exploitation is diminished.

This lifeline renewal through God's amazing grace is what is at the heart of God's sending His Son to bring salvation to those who believe in and receive Him. And it is the reason that from generation to generation each person needs to make his or her own personal decision as to whether or not he or she will receive the covenant of life and forgiveness Christ has made possible for us with God.[1] Now, with that background, step with me into an example of the original splintering.

Cain and Abel were the first two sons born to Adam and Eve (the original Covenant breakers). The problem was that being born into this now-fallen world, they—like their parents—were shaped by the sin-seed's multiplying power.

---

1. If these truths are new or unclear to your understanding, you may turn to Appendix A, "A Prayer for Receiving Christ as Lord and Savior," and Appendix B, "A Prayer for Inviting the Lord to Fill You with the Holy Spirit," anytime during your reading. They provide clarity regarding the way each of us may experience Him and receive the gift of His Son.

Suddenly, *a spirit of separation*—a tendency of their own, as well as a matching evil encouraging it—was at work. By the time we get to the end of the fourth chapter of Genesis, even though only a few generations have gone by, not only has Cain killed his own brother but ensuing generations have begun arguing that such selfish destruction is worthy and wise (see Genesis 4:16–24). The splintering human sin that separated man from God also set forth a cycle that inclines us toward separation in all human relationships, with compounding effects.

The Transmission of Sin

So why do relationships deteriorate—especially in families or with others we deeply care about? If we go to the Source-answer, God's revealed Word given to help us find our way, we learn that it is because all families come from this initial family. The reality of this simple fact is more than interesting. It will help us, as we pray, to understand that human DNA transmits more than just the size and shape of eyes, ears, noses, legs, arms and a host of other physical benefits or problems. Our very "humanness" carries within our makeup a deadly reality: Sin is transmitted to us. This is why you and I and our loved ones are the same in that we are sinners who need a Savior. The degree of our "infestation," our practice of sin, is not the point—I am not intending to condemn or pass judgment on anyone. This is simply to explain the particular dynamic that all relationships are inescapably vulnerable to and why they so often deteriorate and die.

Destructive issues in families are not merely the result of heredity or environment; they trace their roots to Adam and Eve. This calls us to go back to the root for the remedy as well: They accepted God's invitation to re-enter partnership through the Covenant. This gave them the potential for resisting the same "serpent" devices that they first submitted to, and makes possible the reuniting of what has been splintered—or "cut off," to use another analogy.

Relational problems began because the serpent deceived and blinded—he lied and covered the truth. The chain reaction of cutting off people from God, from each other, from commitments and vows, from caring or returning is unending. But so is the power of God's grace and mercy. He will overthrow the "cut-off syndrome" when faith and prayer lay hold of His promises. These beautiful promises declare that God

- can grow life from a dead stump,
- can graft back into the family tree any who have been cut off, and
- can reconnect to His reality whatever has been severed from us by self-opinionation (a claim on "rights" or righteousness that is often religion-based).

Here are two biblical case studies of what God is able to do in the generic family of humankind, and they apply to our specific families as well. I think this gives us hope to see how God fulfills His Word.

Reaching Past Human Failure

Isaiah 11:1 describes the coming Messiah with these words: "There shall come forth a Rod from the stem of Jesse, and a Branch shall grow out of his roots." Isaiah 53:2 also speaks about a root that grows up: "He shall grow up before Him as a tender plant, and as a root out of dry ground." Literally, these texts are saying that a twig shall grow out of a stump.

Why is it significant that Messianic prophecy mentions Jesse? Jesse was the father of David. In other words, the Lord was referring to His family line. Remember that the Lord said to David: "You shall not fail to have a man on the throne of Israel" (1 Kings 9:5). In other words, God was making the promise that out of the root of David's lineage would come a Messiah who would sit on the throne forever.

Now let's glance forward in Scripture at this family line. Several generations after David we come to a descendant named Zedekiah. He was a king of Judah, and he was wicked. His reign was, in fact, the culmination of a season of wickedness that led to God's judgment of His people: Zedekiah was the last real king of Jerusalem before the Babylonians plundered the city and led its people into captivity. (Two puppet kings followed him.) The Bible says that Zedekiah came under a curse. Literally, he was cut off from God, and the city of Jerusalem was destroyed.

David's line, in terms of having a king on an earthly throne, had come to an end. There were children of Zedekiah, this man who was so far from God, but there was no king as it seemed God had promised David.

And that is the very thing we often see in families. People will say, "Well, my great-grandfather was a very godly man. I can't figure out why now, three generations later, we are often so distanced from each other, and some are so far from God." The reason? The "sin-seed" has proliferated along the way and the blessings of God's meant-to-be "harvest" have been *cut off.* But that is not the end of our possibilities. The rest of the story regarding the apparent end of God's promise to David is this: God reached past the hiatus of kings and introduced a new Seed, the Son of David who is the Lord from heaven, sent to recover—rebirth—all the blessing God intends for people like you and me.

Let this truth grip you with hope: If the promise of God concerning His coming Messiah, His own Son, was interrupted by the failure of humanity (in this case, the later generations of David's offspring) and God bridged and reconnected that "cut-off," then He wants us to understand this as a power-principle for prayer. Just as God navigated that failure and brought the tender plant out of the stump that had been cut off, so He is inviting you to pray and believe that He will do the same in your relationships. So let faith arise, knowing if God could bring the fulfillment of His promise into a scene that had actually been cursed by man's rebellion, then there is no member of our families who is beyond the promise of God's Word. Through that One—Jesus the Savior—who rose beyond that stump, He can touch your family tree, wherever it is dead, and bring resurrection life. It is the promise of the Word of God forecast in the Person of Jesus Himself.

Restored from Self-Righteous Presuppositions

A second case of God's truth and power restoring what has been "cut off" is seen as the prophet John the Baptist faced the pride of the Pharisees.

The Pharisees were a dominant band of religionists who, among other things, eventually spearheaded the murder of Jesus on the cross. This scene occurred about four years earlier. They prided themselves on being "children of Abraham," basing their righteousness on their heritage. John had choice words for them.

After calling them a "brood of vipers"—words he used to indicate their attitudes and hateful ways, and which served as evidence of the serpent's sin-seed dominating them—he addressed their error: "Do not think to say to yourselves, 'We have Abraham as our father.' For I say to you that God is able to raise up children to Abraham from these stones. And even now the ax is laid to the root of the trees" (Matthew 3:9–10). He was challenging their supposition that religious beliefs and family history made them right, and in doing so added, "The ax is being laid to the root." He was declaring dramatically that the seed they championed was planted in Satan's lies, and that they had lost the true light of Abraham's faith—growing instead into a tree of pride, self-opinion and tradition that was doomed.

As John preached this message, we know that it became a turning point for some who heard him. Among them, two of the highest ranking Pharisees came to Christ—Nicodemus, who learned what it meant to be "born again" (see John 3), and Joseph of Arimathea, the man who honored Jesus by providing his family tomb as the Lord's burial place (see John 19:38–42).

These two men provide evidence of God's promise that what is cut off can be reconnected—grafted back into His family tree—and that the power of such promises is not for a few, but for all who pray! It is awesome to realize that the first became an example of discovering true "new life" through faith in Christ, the Messiah, and the second donated the tomb that showcased the timeless testimony that Christ is alive forevermore, that death could not hold Him, and that the power of His dying for us is still in effect and available!

I offer the evidence of these two case studies, through which God speaks prophetically about our own situations, as a beginning point of promise for our hearts to embrace when we pray for our loved ones. When it is difficult to pray for those whose openness toward Christ seems hopeless, review these cases where God's promises unfold to us, and hear God's Word say, "I am able to resurrect life from a dead stump; I am able to graft back in what has been cut off; I am able to break through pride."

And if God can do this in *any* setting that reveals the original splintering, He will do it in our families as well.

3

WAR AGAINST THE SPIRIT OF SEPARATION

And they sang a new song, saying: "You are worthy to take the scroll, and to open its seals; for You were slain, and have redeemed us to God by Your blood out of every tribe and tongue and people and nation, and have made us kings and priests to our God; and we shall reign on the earth."

Revelation 5:9–10

As you pray for your loved ones, please never forget that every time you pray you are wrestling for their deliverance from a spirit—an evil influence loose in the world named Satan, who still practices his skills of blinding and binding that he may deceive and destroy.

Do not allow the mention of the devil to resonate within you as immature or as superstitious, as though he is less than real or that it is childish even to bother with such thoughts. Not only is the Bible very clear about his existence, it warns us about his intentions and exposes his tactics. Equally, if you believe in the reality of Satan's existence, don't be intimidated, for the Bible is also clear in saying we need not cower at the thought of his works or power. Jesus Christ is the One who conquered the devil's capacity to dominate any life or situation. That means that when we put our faith in Him—the Risen Lord—we are partners in His triumph and have the privilege of not only *living* in His victory but *enforcing* and *advancing* it. So it is in that light that I want to help us understand the battle over that advancing. We may recognize that praying for those we love calls us to have faith for the answer, but sometimes it also means engaging in an invisible war. Many situations will involve prayer for dear ones who are not only needy but also bound or blinded. Those confining cords or blinders are the result of either their cooperation with or their exposure to influences beyond themselves.

This chapter deals with this subject not as a mystical matter but as a factual one. And when you understand that you are in a battle, when it becomes fixed in your mind, you will have a clearer viewpoint

- on a person's attitude, and why it seems so obtuse;
- on a person's present situation and why it seems fixed, as though the individual is trapped even while thinking he or she is free; and
- on how that person treats you, and why he or she seems so hostile.

This understanding will begin to enlighten you when facing seemingly futile or hopeless situations, helping you to get your eyes off the problem or the person and onto the fact that he or she is blinded and bound and manipulated by the powers of darkness. Get that fixed firmly in your mind and it will change your whole stance in prayer. You will begin to realize that you are in a spiritual wrestling match, not a relational one.

Second Corinthians 4:3–4 says this:

> But even if our gospel is veiled, it is veiled to those who are perishing, whose minds the god of this age has blinded, who do not believe, lest the light of the gospel of the glory of Christ, who is the image of God, should shine on them.

This does not have to do with trying to lick your older brother, whom you could never beat up. It does not have to do with changing your dad's mind, who is so stubborn he will never budge. It does not have to do with your close friend, who could not care less. It does not have to do with any of that. You are not wrestling flesh and blood; you are dealing with the blindness the devil brings. The god of this age has blinded those who are outside of Christ.

When you begin to wonder why people close to you disobey God or live the way they do, when you become despairing and brokenhearted because they never pay attention to what you have to say, remember that the spirit of disobedience is working in them. We who are Adam's offspring were all once that way (see Ephesians 2:1–3)—very much like puppets with the enemy pulling the strings. But the whole picture clears when we see things clearly and learn to discern that not only are many for whom we pray lost, they are also blinded and bound. Their disobedience to God allows the bondage to deepen and their strings to be pulled by an evil puppeteer.

Arguing with them doesn't help; that is the same as trying to convince a blind person to see. Our primary place is on our knees—to pray and know that eventually the light will come to those eyes. Jesus can cut the strings of their bondage by the power of His Word as we pray, calling on Him to begin the advance of His Kingdom of light and power into their souls and circumstances.

As we pray for salvation for our loved ones, we see thus far that within the covenant of God we can lay claim to two key promises. The first is that after the man and woman sinned in the Garden, Father God set in motion a plan of salvation through Jesus Christ to overrule the curse they unleashed on themselves. The second is that God can bring resurrection life to any part of any family that has been splintered as a result of the Fall.

This brings us to a further promise: He who comes to dwell in you and me is sufficient to override whatever cursed works of hell have come upon any members of our families. This is vital to realize as we learn to deal with a spirit of death and separation. Let's look at the essence of this battle.

The Primary Effect

We begin by seeing how the sin-seed inclines the fallen nature to give place to the devil (see Ephesians 4:27) and the impact this has upon personal relationships. Turning again to the introduction of sin into the human race, let's assess what happened with Adam and Eve and their offspring. We turn here because it is exactly what occurs time and again in families as the Fall's ongoing impact on the entire human race continues like a string of dominoes falling forward on one another, generation to generation. Every sin proceeding from the original separation from God holds the potential for ongoing separation through the whole family tree of mankind.

In the third and fourth chapters of Genesis we see in the first family this scenario: Male and female believed the serpent's lie. They disobeyed God, partook of the forbidden fruit and fell. When the Lord came to them and asked why they had disobeyed Him, the man said, "The woman You gave to me, she gave me of the fruit and I ate."

Here is the pattern that was established:

- The devil's lie was believed (deception).
- The forbidden fruit was eaten (sin).
- Adam blamed his mate for the sin (accusation).

"The woman You gave me," i.e., *"God, this is not really my fault; it's hers!"* The initial exchange that took place after the Fall in the first family's relationship involved *accusation.* This was just the beginning of manifestation of the spirit of separation and death. By *manifestation* I refer to external evidence of invisible realities. It is a dynamic of evil that, after our human willfulness and disobedience leave us naked and vulnerable, it is able to reinforce that willfulness and eventually manipulate us—just as if you or I were to start a trip in a car only to have the wheel taken over by an intruder. The Bible describes this as actually giving turf—literally handing over to another property belonging to you—and it does not

apply only to non-believers. Ephesians 4:25–32 describes ways that believers can willfully, though ignorantly, allow the strength of evil influence to have a place in their lives by stepping outside the boundaries of the strong defense we have in Christ.

Another manifestation in the Garden was a spirit of *competition* where the desire to be in charge came into play. When God spoke these words to Eve, "Your desire shall be for your husband, and he shall rule over you" (Genesis 3:16), the word *desire* was not referring to sexual passion but to the quest to control or "win," as we might say. This spirit of competition—she wants to win; he wants to win—plagues many couples. By it, competition enters every part of a family.

I have seen situations—undoubtedly you have, too—where the spirit of competition is the very thing that keeps people away from Christ. Two brothers have been competitive all their lives, and today the only way one of them can finally win is to refuse what he knows his brother wants—for him to come to Christ. It is the spirit of competition seeking to obstruct his salvation. This is a powerful spirit. Give it no place in your life. Come against it, recognizing it as a manifestation of darkness. Further, it is never overthrown. Consider the brothers in our example. The one brother, the believer, thinks he can out-argue or out-persuade his brother with "in your face" religion. It is only another game of who wins, and only God's Spirit can. The role of brother number one is to pray—but with the power of the Holy Spirit.

We see further workings of sin's separating power to affect children in Genesis 4:2–9, which relates the story of Cain and Abel. The passage describes Cain's *jealousy* and *anger* toward his brother. Later, after he killed Abel, he said to God, "Am I my brother's keeper?" In those words is a manifestation of the sin-seed from his parents. Further refusing to accept responsibility for his brother also reveals *rejection* and *desertion*. Presuming he had no responsibility for his brother, he not only had no use for him but found a way to be done with him.

Flavor, Warmth and Radiance

These expressions of the spirit of separation and death distilling from the Fall are not unusual. They are everywhere present along with many others. They are as real today as then and as powerful in their destructive capability. The question for us becomes how we will respond. We can either let these traits infect us and block the flow of divine life into our relationships, or we can become a leavening influence by purging ourselves of them and praying against them.

Second Corinthians 2:16 says that we can be a fragrance of "life leading to life" in Christ. Matthew 5:13–14 says that we are salt and light, bringing flavor as well as warmth and radiance by our places in families. These personal dynamics affect the spiritual battle, revealing how our lives as well as our prayers penetrate the battle scene; how fragrance, flavor and warmth reach our loved ones at a human level while our prayers melt down spiritual resistance through the Holy Spirit.

Let's learn more, as we pray, about how our part in the answer is to show genuine care for the *person* we love, and abandon ill-timed and pushy efforts at evangelism. I would never argue against the fact that the Holy Spirit knows the right time for you to testify graciously to the truth of Jesus Christ. Generally we recognize this time because of obvious interest shown by a needy loved one. I never want to discourage you from speaking the Word of the Gospel clearly and leading people to the Lord. But there is also great lack of wisdom at times when we fail to recognize that our words are spoken too hastily, given before the soil is prepared to receive them. Unless God's Spirit is at work working to break through Satan's obstacles, we are not going to bear any fruit.

If we are going to begin praying redemptively for our families, we can learn to become a presence of grace as well as an instrument of overcoming prayer, letting Christ's spirit of resurrection life flow through us freely to those we love.

Here are ways to begin.

Let the Holy Spirit shine a searchlight in your own heart and cleanse anything that restricts the power and liberty of your intercessory role in the family.

I know that I am neutralized for effective prayer to the degree that negativity characterizes my attitude toward anyone for whom I pray. In a moment, I will relate how I was surprised when the Holy Spirit showed me that I had an attitude of criticism toward a family member. I had to face the strong likelihood that I myself might have been an obstruction to the spiritual release I longed for. Let me ask you: Do you have an attitude of accusation or criticism toward any family member of your own? You want him to be saved, but he irritates you so much! The Lord Jesus wants us to see that we cannot partner with His Holy Spirit for the flow of life into that person while we are giving place to the flow of death.

We need to ask the Lord to bring to our minds—to our understanding by revelation in prayer or by discernment—any ways in which we need to pray against that spirit of separation and death. Let's let go of anything the Holy Spirit shows us of unforgiveness, competition, anger, rejection or jealousy. After that period we *are* our brothers' (sisters', aunts', cousins' *et al*) keepers!

We refuse to sustain that spirit of death and separation through any kind of "labeling." For example, I have talked with people who sincerely want to see family members brought to Christ, but they ignorantly play to the family's penchant for labeling. I am referring to words that categorize certain members. "Well, Joe has always been like that. . . ." Joe has heard numerous times that he has always been like that, and the power of that label to keep Joe like that is mighty. Or how many times, even in jest, do people say, "She's the black sheep of our family"? The power these names have to perpetuate the spirit of separation and death is incredibly dynamic even if unknown to the person of whom they are spoken. These words bind people and prevent the release of grace toward them.

Further, we let go of our hurts and forgive. In Matthew 18:21–35 Jesus taught the great message of forgiveness in the parable of the unforgiving servant. This servant had been forgiven a great deal, but he was not forgiving in return. If I have preached a sermon from Matthew 18 once, I have preached from it a hundred times—on every continent and in every kind of situation. It is difficult to be brief on this topic, but I want to note just this one thing. In this story, Jesus taught the principle that our having been forgiven means that we must be equally forgiving ourselves. We have no right to sit in judgment on anyone. If we refuse to release the spirit of forgiveness, we chain people more than we can ever know.

Also, be consistent to sustain your loved ones in prayer. By withholding our prayers, we withhold life. Lift up prayer that is passionately *loving* and willing to continue in patience, waiting for the harvest of your loved one's soul the same way Father God is patiently waiting for the harvest of multitudes in this old world (see James 5:7).

We need to be open to the Holy Spirit's direct confrontation, becoming willing to look honestly at each of these things. As we are purged of them we can be released into more effective prayer. Without such integrity of heart before God we may unwittingly be preventing our families and friends from receiving the flow of God's life and love.

When Motivation Gets in the Way

One of the primary lessons I learned about these truths—especially unforgiveness—had to do with a near relative. As you read on, note my failure to recognize my own responsibility to be as forgiving toward others as God has been to me. I have often felt that I erected an obstacle to a loved one's salvation. Let me tell you why.

My dear wife, Anna, and I have a total of nine siblings between us and a number of cousins, many of whom needed Christ. Frank was one of them. Many years ago at a family homecoming I distinctly sensed that Frank was avoiding me. To some degree I was not surprised; he knew I was preparing for a lifetime of Gospel ministry as a pastor. Since he had a Christian background, one from which he had distanced himself while in the military, I felt he was giving me a fairly wide berth, presuming I might "nail him with the Gospel."

When I sensed this distancing, I made up my mind that I was going to try to win his friendship. I then devised a plan. Knowing of his interest in bowling, I took my opportunity when our paths crossed at the sandwich table at a family gathering. "Hey, Frank," I said, smiling warmly. "Anna and I are in town for the next week. How about let's go down to the alleys and roll a couple of lines. What do you think?"

He was obviously taken aback—first because he didn't know I had come up behind him, and second because I am sure he did not think I cared to spend any time with him. He groped for words, possibly wishing for an excuse, and then said, "Uh, I'll have to check my schedule and give you a call."

He never did. And from that time—no matter how many times I saw Frank—I thought something along these lines: *If he's not interested in me, I'm not going to push myself on him. Let him have it his own way.* I was a lot younger in my life with things to learn. This was in some ways simply the kind of thing a "guy" does.

Some twenty years passed. I saw Frank at similar family events, usually spaced five years apart. Our kids grew up at the same time; his daughter Francey and our daughter Becky developed a friendship that they maintained by writing regularly to each other.

It was our daughters' contact that would occasion one of my most significant encounters with myself. It was clearly God's providence and goodness to me, but it brought me face-to-face with unforgiveness and the way it can lie undetected, breeding hardness in the heart of anyone—even a pastor who had no idea he (that's *me*) had been hardened against a loved one, and who, if asked, would have hastened to say he wanted to see that individual come to Christ. Here is what happened.

It was Valentine's Day, a Sunday morning, and I was up early as always. Anna and the kids were still sleeping, but I wanted to spend time reviewing my message.

I crossed the kitchen, and, while opening the refrigerator to get the milk for some cereal, I saw a Valentine on the kitchen table. The picture and words on the front of the card were humorous, and I opened it to read the punch line. Those are words I will never remember, because as I laughed at the joke I noted it was from Francey to our Becky. Glancing briefly I caught the brief note: "Becky, thank you for your note to me, saying that you pray for my dad's salvation every day."

I am not being melodramatic when I say that if you had taken an icicle and driven it through my heart I could not have felt more frozen. I literally staggered the three steps into our dining room and fell on the floor, suddenly seized by shame, embarrassment and repentance. Three things hit me all at once: I could not remember praying for Frank for *years*; God had had to touch my daughter's tender heart to awaken prayer for that loved one in my place; and I cried out to God to forgive me for the blindness and hardness that had evolved in my soul over my sense of Frank's rejection of my efforts at friendship.

It is enough to say I was changed by the moment. I presume you understand that I had not been conscious of my prayerless "counter-rejection" of him. And it is certain that I got the point: Frank became large on my prayer agenda, especially because my repentance for my unwitting indifference blossomed into an opposite, genuinely new love for my relative.

The following August on a Sunday night Anna and I had just arrived home from our little church—well before The Church On The Way became the massive congregation God caused it to become. It had been a hot day, and there was no air-conditioning in our little building. I immediately went into our bathroom to shower. Anna went into the kitchen to prepare us and our four children a Sunday night snack. I had just finished showering and putting on a bathrobe when the phone rang. Anna and I both picked up receivers where we were, and I sat down on the edge of the bed as I said, "Hello." It was Frank, and he immediately got to the point after we greeted each other.

"Guys, I just wanted to call you tonight without waiting, because I knew you'd want to be the first to know. Tonight I gave my heart to Jesus!" He was understandably jubilant. Anna and I joined him in praising the Lord simultaneously, then we spoke a few minutes and the call concluded.

I lay down on the bed and began to cry—and they were tears of praise, but they were also flavored with the remembrance of my prayerlessness for a time I could not measure. While my indifference toward him had not been a calculated reaction, I would later receive insight into a frightening possibility in Jesus' parable of the unforgiving servant in Matthew 18:21–35. The naked truth He exposed is the tragic capability of someone who has been forgiven not relaying that spirit toward others. It is unwarranted, since we *all* have received God's forgiveness far more than we can measure. The text leaves an image to be pondered by our souls: The forgiven servant leaves his fellow servant in a prison cell, *solely on the grounds of the offense he feels!*

The message is pointed and can be incriminating. In the Lord's Prayer we ask God to forgive us our sins (trespasses) as we forgive those who sin against us. Jesus also said, "If you are going to worship Me and you remember you have a stressed relationship, leave your gift at the altar and go first to be restored to your brother" (see Matthew 5:23–24).

Without question, among our greatest challenges in praying for those we love is not allowing our hearts to be wearied and worn or to become a place of unwitting hardness as we pray, "Until. . . ."

When the "until" seems long, let the rain of God's promises refresh you by His Spirit. His Word is true and the length of time does not mean there are no advances being made by God's providence and angel workings.

Let me leave you with my contemporary phrasing of Arthur Hugh Clough's (1819–1861) poem "Say Not the Struggle Naught Availeth."

Lift Up Your Eyes

Don't say, "Our struggle's not prevailing."
Nor say our work and pain won't gain;
Nor say, "The enemy's not failing,
And as things have been, things remain!"

But say, "Our hopes don't lie, our fears do!"
And know within that smoke concealed
Your fellow-warriors have a breakthrough,
And but for you possess the field.

40

And when the tide seems slow in growing,
And here appears so spent in strength.
Still, from the heights a river's flowing
To join that tide and spread its length.

For not through eastward windows only
Do we invite the morning light.
In front the sun may climb so slowly,
But westward, Look! The land is bright!

Adapted by Jack W. Hayford

4

Doing Your Part and Letting God Do His

Another parable He put forth to them, saying: "The kingdom of heaven is like a mustard seed, which a man took and sowed in his field, which indeed is the least of all the seeds; but when it is grown it is greater than the herbs and becomes a tree, so that the birds of the air come and nest in its branches." Another parable He spoke to them: "The kingdom of heaven is like leaven, which a woman took and hid in three measures of meal till it was all leavened."

Matthew 13:31–33

We have just seen that when it comes to ministering the saving life of Jesus to our loved ones, we can block the Lord's life-flow by our unperceived but unproductive attitudes. Now I want to show you that our best intentions to "do good" with a pure heart can also sabotage that work!

The problem is this: Notwithstanding the power and necessity of prayer, we are entirely capable of getting in the Lord's way. We can pray and then turn right around and mess things up. I think all of us have had experiences of doing that. We shudder at the thought of doing it again, but the deep, deep emotional commitment and involvement we have with loved ones makes us all the more vulnerable to doing the wrong thing after we have prayed the right way.

Now we advance our theme of praying our loved ones into the family of God, but before we move further into our discussion of how we *pray* for them we need the companion teaching of how we *relate* to them. Essentially, this has to do with ministry. Because some confuse that word with *ministers* in the sense of church leadership, let me broaden the concept of ministry as it relates to the disciples of Jesus.

Ministry refers to "living out" the qualities of Jesus' character—His love and forgiveness toward others, His servant ways and His Spirit-empowered works in daily personal relationships. It is about transmitting the full dimension of the saving life of Jesus. We want to discuss this in the light of two parables. In these pictures we see how faith affects the advance or fruitfulness of God's will, Word and ways, the entry of His Kingdom, which drives out sin's darkness, bondage and death. The pivotal thing we will see is how they call us to an active part in the process but also help us avoid presuming we can fulfill God's part. If we can receive our Lord's ministry principles in these passages, I know we will find balance and wisdom for our confident expectation of seeing our loved ones come to Christ.

I felt drawn to Matthew 13:31–33 as I was preparing a series of messages for our congregation under the titles "Praying Your Family into God's Kingdom" and "Loving the Kingdom into Your Family." Let's look at the truths presented in these verses. The parables about a man planting a tiny mustard seed that becomes a great tree and then about a woman who places a bit of leaven in three measures of meal are laden with insight. (Leaven, incidentally, refers to yeast, which when placed in bread dough causes it to rise.)

In these texts, Jesus is talking about the introduction of God's rule into persons or places where His Kingdom has not been before. He gives a picture of a man in a field and a woman in her kitchen. That seems very significant to me; both are in the everydayness of their lives. And what each one does is a relatively small but very essential thing. The man picks up *a single seed*. This is not at all like the farmer who goes out to sow and casts seeds widely and broadly. Here the sower takes *one tiny seed* and plants it carefully, intentionally; in other words, he puts it in an atmosphere it can grow in, and it does—growing into a great tree. The woman puts *a little yeast* into the dough, and it penetrates the whole loaf, for experience has taught her that otherwise the dough will not rise but will be dense and flat.

The first point we discern from Jesus' lesson is that, from the human side, both an action toward God and an action toward life's realities must be balanced. In any potentially life- or truth-giving situation we have a part that is essential and that stems from our desire and our practical understanding. Then, from that point, we reach our limit in bringing the growth (as with the seed) or the rise and eventual softness (as the yeast produces in the bread). These natural or chemical processes in the parables reflect invisible realities that only the power of God's life-giving ways can achieve.

I love this imagery because neither of the things that the man and the woman do is dramatic. He plants a small seed; she takes a little yeast. And with that, something of the miraculous—or beyond human ability—happens. After the man sows the seed, essentially his work is done. The sunshine and rain come from the hand of God; the life in the seed is inherent. Regarding the yeast, chemical action takes over. The woman does not have to come and attach something to the dough to inflate it. She does her little bit, and it goes from there.

It is quite appropriate to apply this imagery to our families and close friends, it seems to me, because both of these are very home-related pictures. The man is probably working in a field next to his house, and the woman is obviously in her kitchen. What Jesus is indicating is how the Kingdom enters and eventually takes over when people like us do what we can do—but do it with the practical sensitivity they did.

Just as a realm (such as soil) needs to be prepared with care, so there are ways we can relate to our loved ones that will assist their receptivity—but this must be done with care for them as people of value rather than prospects for our soul-winning victory. Similarly, the cook needs to give the yeast time to puff up and *soften* the dough. Yet how many times do we move in haste, hardening the hearts of those we want to see brought to life in Jesus? The outcome—a living tree and a flavorful loaf (bread is a biblical type of humanity)—*does* indicate the result of human action, wisely partnering with practical principles, but it also reminds us

46

of the limits of our abilities and the need to allow both the time and the space for God's divine workings.

Zechariah 4:6 is often quoted as a prophetic direction to look to the Lord: "Not by might nor by power, but by My Spirit." This verse is not intended to imply that there is nothing we are to do; rather, it is a reminder that we cannot—in any way possible—get the job done. It is also a reminder that while being consistent to do *our* part we need to be careful not to get in the way of God's doing His—or worse, trying to do His part on our own.

We are surely wise, however, to recognize that the man and woman doubtless took steps to *protect* what was planted and placed, but they did not try to *push*! The planter would have put a shield around the place he planted the seed so it would not be trampled. The woman would have put a cloth over the dough to retain its moisture. Our prayer for our loved ones involves such wisdom, because when the seed of truth is sown in human hearts, then demons like birds will try to steal it, as we saw in an earlier parable, or people with insensitivity in relating to the unbelieving can crush it. Moreover, the moistness of a human soul is the result of "prayer cover," which sustains an atmosphere that will enable the dynamic of God's Spirit to "give rise" to greater readiness for answering God's call.

Praying for those we love is not a substitute for their need to hear God's Word of truth—the Gospel. But many of those we find resisting already know it, and for them the "pushiness" of a relative deepens resistance. On the other hand—as you abide in continual prayer—the truth that they may most need at the present is a sense of your acceptance of them, even as they understand that acceptance is not approval of sinful behavior. While it is painful to see a loved one persist in sin, especially if it is self-destructive, God's Spirit has spoken or is speaking to them about their need to turn to Him. *Our prayer for them is pivotal in this regard. But it is also our job to leave God's part for Him to achieve, as only He can.*

5

BASIC PROMISES
TO APPLY

So they said, "Believe on the Lord Jesus Christ, and you will be saved, and your household."

Acts 16:31

There is hope in your future, says the LORD, that your children shall come back to their own border.

Jeremiah 31:17

Wives, likewise, be submissive [biblically respectful] to your own husbands, that even if some do not obey the word, they, without a word, may be won by the conduct of their wives.

1 Peter 3:1

Look with me now at three pertinent passages that teach us about bringing our loved ones into the heavenly Kingdom. They hold faith-inspiring insight that, as we receive and live in their promises, will help us not get in the Lord's way as we continue to pray.

Let's draw the following from each biblical passage given above: from the first, the power of God's promises; from the second, help to avoid being trapped in hopelessness; and from the third, deepening our sense of the importance of our own behavior. All are inescapably significant if we would effectively pray for those we love. They show how the Kingdom enters and eventually takes over.

The Promise for Your Household

The Bible speaks to us often of the penetration of the power of the Kingdom of God into our homes and families. Acts 16:31 is probably one of the most quoted verses in the Bible—certainly the one quoted most often when it comes to the expectation in our hearts that our families will be brought to the Lord. This Scripture shows the power at work when belief is present in just one individual in a family.

Acts 16 relates an incident regarding Paul and Silas, who have just broached the European continent with the Gospel. They have been cast into a Philippian prison because of the events surrounding the deliverance of a slave girl who was demon-possessed. This young woman was a fortuneteller—she had a spirit of divination—and her masters gained a certain income from exploiting her dubious gift. When Paul cast out the spirit, her masters saw that their hope of making profit from her was gone. They incited a multitude against Paul and Silas, which had them beaten and thrown into prison.

At midnight Paul and Silas, with their feet in stocks, were singing hymns and praying when suddenly a great earthquake occurred. "All the doors were opened and everyone's chains were loosed" (Acts 16:26). The keeper of the prison awoke and supposed the prisoners had fled. He was ready to kill himself, because his life would be taken anyway by his superior officers for dereliction of duty, but Paul cried out for him not to harm himself because all were still present.

The jailer came running with a light into the inner dungeon. Trembling, he fell down before them and said, "Sirs, what must I do to be saved?" Obviously, some conversation had taken place between Paul, Silas and that jailer. He did not just come up with those words out of the sky. He perceived that there was something more to life that he did not know about. Verse 31 is the answer Paul and Silas gave: "They said, 'Believe on the Lord Jesus Christ, and you will be saved, you and your household.'"

Further we read:

> Then they spoke the word of the Lord to him and to all who were in his house. And he took them the same hour of the night and washed their stripes. And immediately he and all his family were baptized. Now when he had brought them into his house, he set food before them; and he rejoiced, having believed in God with all his household.
>
> Acts 16:32–34

The beauty of this story is not only the man's conversion, but the fact that his whole family was brought to Christ the same day by the impact of what had happened in his own life. We could only wish that that would be exactly the timing for all of our families when we come to the Lord! Even though the timing is not the same, however, the truth is the same.

Listen again. The Bible says: "Believe on the Lord Jesus Christ, and you will be saved, you and your household." The promise of the Word is that we as individuals may expect that what God has done in our lives will infuse the lives of those we touch. In the same way that the leaven fills the whole loaf, the presence of the leaven of the Kingdom in your life and mine will begin to penetrate our homes. Just as the mustard seed grows into a great tree, so will the seed of Gospel light in us begin to develop through the whole family tree.

The Promise of Return

The next Scripture passage is a beautiful prophecy. It addresses the desire that our children come into the Kingdom.

> Thus says the LORD: "A voice was heard in Ramah, lamentation and bitter weeping, Rachel weeping for her children, refusing to be comforted for her children, because they are no more." Thus says the LORD: "Refrain your voice from weeping, and your eyes from tears; for your work shall be rewarded, says the LORD, and they [that is, your children] shall come back from the land of the enemy. There is hope in your future, says the LORD, that your children shall come back to their own border."
>
> Jeremiah 31:15–17

To the weeping parent whose children could not be found, the Lord said, "Stop crying. Your work shall be rewarded." Your prayers, your sowing of the seed, your introduction of the leaven will be rewarded. Your children shall come again from the land of the enemy and enter into their own border.

We will talk a great deal more, by the way, about praying for children in chapters 6 and 9.

The Promise of Potential

The third passage is another instance of awesome potential for the praying believer who does just the little bit that is his part. We will be talking more extensively about the relationship between husbands and wives in the next chapter, but I want to address here briefly the aspect of promise in 1 Peter 3.

This chapter of Scripture begins with a case of direct address to wives. The husbands do not escape requirements without accountability either. Verse 7 has enough material to keep them occupied. In fact, one day I spent about an hour and a half with the men in our church's men's growth seminar on this verse alone! There is a lot of thunder to get the guys straightened out, too.

But here the Scripture is speaking to the wives. Be in subjection, or in submission, or in a right-ordered relationship to your husbands, verse 1 says, so "that even if some [husbands] do not obey the word, they, without a word, may be won by the conduct of their wives." This verse is almost offensive to some dear believers who profess that the only way to witness is to "get the Word into their hearts." Their habits are based on two suppositions: first, that their hearers have not already heard it (and certainly not as well as they can "lay it on"), and, second, that "witnessing" is accomplished solely by a verbal presentation.

The ancient preacher St. Francis of Assisi is quoted as saying this: "Always preach the Gospel—and when necessary, use words." He obviously believed, as we wisely should, that God's Word becomes incarnate through us when we allow the Holy Spirit to reveal the character, charisma, sensitivity and grace of our Lord Jesus Christ. So, of course! The Word of God is present here in the behavior of the wife this text describes. The message asserts that if wives whose husbands do not know Christ will live in a sensitive, loving, pure, self-giving and godly relationship with them, it will lead to their salvation.

Qualities of the Kingdom with its resident power will transmit even though no word about it is spoken—it will be evident in their conduct. In other words, reaching an unsaved husband is not accomplished by parroting Bible verses or goading him to go to church. I am not proposing it as a strategy, but I know one woman who, never losing her passion for Christ or His Word during the season of time involved, would not go to church during the years her husband had stepped back on his earlier commitment to Christ. It was a case involving a longer story, and when she told it to me I commended her for her wisdom—even before he returned to the Lord. It was a matter of believing or disbelieving the Word of God in the text above: She believed it and proved its promise, but not without living out its expectations of her.

I believe there are numerous men who avoid the Lord in their outward behavior, but who are not successfully escaping His voice in their inner soul. How His partners represent the Father during such times—irrespective of gender or domestic status—will without doubt be effective as the Holy

Spirit erodes their barriers to belief or commitment. Let's teach and live the dynamic that abounds within and around the truth we are discussing here!

The Next Step

These three passages of Scripture regarding the penetration of the power of the Kingdom of God into our homes and families are lovely. The first one says with certainty that "you will be saved, you and your household." The requirement is *believe*. Believe in the Lord Jesus Christ—not just "believe and get saved" but "believe in the Lord Jesus Christ and believe for your house."

The second word includes a promise also, a promise of return: "Your children will return from the land of the enemy." Whatever drifting has happened with family members, they will return.

In the third word we see awesome potential. It says that people who are not obeying the Word may be won by the character of a believing spouse.

These are promises in the Word of God—the leaven that can introduce God's rule into persons or places where His Kingdom has not been before. Now how do we get the leaven into the dough? By the patterns in our walk as we meet various kinds of people. That is the subject of our next chapter.

6

Promises and Patterns for Reaching People

Let your speech always be with grace, seasoned with salt,
that you may know how you ought to answer each one.

Colossians 4:6

Living in the Kingdom means straightening out our relationships; too often we make a mess of things with our
overactive good intentions. We fail to let the leaven do its
work, or we poke and prod the tiny mustard seed until its
potential for growth is stunted.

As we stand on the promises of Scripture, we need also to
understand right patterns of living in our key relationships.
Let's look, then, at four categories in which we can have more
effective patterns in our walk and better ways of relating.

The first is husbands and wives, then older children, then the younger children and then relatives.

Husbands and Wives

Here are a few scenarios that are not that unusual when one spouse is a believer and one is not:

- "I'm leaving for church, now—wish I didn't have to go alone. See you later." Remember, guilt motivation is always loveless. (Repeat that phrase five times.)
- "Hmm. I think I'll just leave my Bible here on his/her newspaper. Maybe he/she will open it out of curiosity, thinking I left it accidentally." (Fat chance.)
- "I know you want to go to sleep, honey, but I need the light on so I can read my Bible a little longer. I feel like such a new person now!" (Then why not show a little consideration and go to bed!)

In contrast, the way to "win by your conduct" is to use good sense, such as thoughtful acts, loving sensitivity, sexual responsiveness, small surprises. With this, settle into a long-range pursuit of personal growth as a Christian *person* rather than as the household's *preacher*. Apply the simple principles below. They are what 1 Peter 3:1 is calling you to, and as you live it, Christ-in-you will shine the same beauty that drew lost people to Him everywhere He went. As He is "lifted up" in your lifestyle, He will draw your spouse to Himself, too (see John 12:32).

1. Grow your relationship with God, seeing it is well ordered.

2. Make time to feed on and then relate rightly to His Word daily.
3. Learn how to relate with openness to the ministry of the Holy Spirit. He is the Spirit of Wisdom and will help you in practical ways—relationally, domestically and spiritually.

Clearly the path of biblical winsomeness that wins is that the believing spouse live a real, loving, unpretentious life—the kind that in very practical ways characterizes God's Kingdom rule in a person's life. If not announced, it simply becomes "infectious reality." Your choice to take the route of faith rather than the path of religiousness is the shortest way to the destiny you seek for your unsaved wife or husband: It will literally take over that person without one sermon being preached, without one tract being read, without one verse being quoted and without one "surprise" TV program cleverly being tuned into. It happens because there is something of the "takeover" presence of the Kingdom happening in you, and a spouse can tell it.

It is painful to encounter sincere women or men who have tried to goad their mates to God. That style shows in the set of the person's countenance. It is taut, not tender; words are syrupy, not sweet; and "spiritual" becomes sickening, not attractive.

I was speaking at a conference in New Mexico when a woman came up to me who looked like the stereotype of what I will call the classical "highly religious" woman. She really was not an unappealing woman, but she had managed to do about everything she could do to become other than that, with her hair drawn back rather severely and her stark dress (you could see she could afford something more feminine but she possibly thought that would be unspiritual). I am not one to invite people to embrace "being fashionable" for the sake of carnal appeal or proving they're "cool." But it was sad to see an interpretation of spirituality that argued against its vitality and meaning.

She looked up at me and in a tone that I can only describe as "prissy" said, "Pastor Hayford, we're so delighted to have you ministering here in our city. It's been excellent teaching. I feel that I would like to have you pray for my husband's salvation."

I hurt for that lady, as I perceived her tone and slightly elevated air of spiritual superiority. As I paused to respond, I believe the Holy Spirit gave me a word of wisdom. I reached out and took her hand as I said with a gentle and pleasant tone, "You know I'd be glad to do that, but before we do, I sense that the Lord has given me something to say to you.

"I believe," I continued, "that I'm to say to you that the Lord wants you to forgive your husband for not being a believer."

She looked at me, dumbfounded. Forgive someone for not being a believer in Jesus? I then gave her a Bible verse to help her understand the point, Romans 5:8—a verse I had never considered having the implications I was seeing in it at that moment.

"You know, 'forgiving us for not being saved' is what the Father did for you and me: *'God demonstrates His own love toward us, in that while we were still sinners, Christ died for us.'* It was *that* very willingness of His to openly show His readiness to accept us first, even while we had no heart toward Him, as we were, that made it possible for us to be moved by His love to receive Him, with all He desired to give us."

She looked shell-shocked and not particularly pleased at the word I brought her. But I said I would pray as she requested.

She allowed me to pray for her, and as I did I expressed to the Lord my sense of honor for her faithfulness to and spiritual concern for her husband over those many years. Afterward, I was not hard on her, but gently implored her to weigh a reality the Holy Spirit showed me she needed to confront: that her longtime disappointment with her husband's refusing Christ had worn her patience to the nub. In fact, though I did not say it to her, it was clear that *she was mad at her husband for being unsaved!* Yes, her disappointment of years was surely understandable, and I did feel patient in her behalf—honoring toward the times she had doubtless had to "go it alone" because he would not follow her pursuit of Christ. But I also recognized there was likely more to the case than anyone knew, and that my words had been a confrontation by God's Spirit—one given in love, and not with insensitivity.

When we finished the prayer, she turned away quickly— no tears, no comments but a formal "Thank you." She seemed more braced to persist in her frustration at that moment, but by God's grace I would hope soon to discover she received God's prompting—and possibly a fruitful result of what clearly needed to be a better relationship with her husband.

I cannot help but believe there is a foundational principle there for our ministry to all of our loved ones. I have never experienced the pain and the torment of being in a home where a spouse is estranged from what is so priceless and precious to you. I do not want to seem ungracious in any way on that point, but I know that you never win anything by being bitter over the fact that someone has not yet come to the Lord. These ones need to be loved, and that love takes very, very practical dimensions.

I believe that the Lord Jesus would have us show the quality of patience that the Father is showing toward them—with gentleness and goodness and consistency in that patience and love. Then, even if years go by and they do not receive the Lord, the leaven is still working in the bread. It is giving rise all the time to something in them: the awareness that the Kingdom has come to their home.

Some of the dearest women that I have ever met in my life are women who have walked for decades with Jesus, and whose husbands have not come to the Lord—sometimes until right up to the end of their lives. You wonder how on earth a man could be resistant to the love of God, having seen it so beautifully modeled in a woman like that. I cannot promise that this will bring instant conversion, but the Bible does promise that it will happen. It requires consideration and love and patience.

The same idea is communicated in 1 Corinthians 7:10–16 in another context. The apostle Paul was dealing with marital problems in the Corinthian church. Corinth was a hellhole. There is no question that that city was the finest expression of the Pit that you could find on the surface of the earth in the time of the New Testament Church. Out of that debased and debauched culture, people were coming to Jesus and being changed by the transforming power of God.

There were many cases, however, in which people were being saved but their spouses were remaining wrapped up in the paganism around them. The apostle told them to stay with their unsaved spouses because a penetration of Kingdom life would take hold of them.

Let me again mention this point. By telling these believers that the unbelieving husband is sanctified by the believing wife and vice versa, Paul was not saying that this saves them. He was likely addressing the question of whether or not a believing spouse is "contaminated" by the impurity of an unbelieving spouse who participates in the sins and immorality of the culture. The answer is no. Paul said, basically, "If he (or she) is willing to stay with you, hang in there because there is a godly influence that does not allow one person to be made impure because of the actions of another—and he (or she) may be brought to the light."

Now Paul did say that if an unbelieving partner will not stay committed to the marriage and leaves, the believer is free to leave as well, but this does not work the other way around.

I got a question this week about this very topic. Someone wrote and asked, "Why doesn't your church let wives file for divorce?" After every effort has been made with couples through pastoral council with biblical instruction, practical guidance and spiritual ministry (including an errant spouse who is passive or persistent in violating the biblical requirements of marriage) we take a stand. While we never prevent anyone from filing for divorce, neither do we encourage it.[1]

1. The increasing cases of spousal abuse—violence from an increasingly paganized culture—require the church's firm stand to assure the protection of either a wife or a

We also urge, unless it is impractical given a particular situation, that if an unbelieving spouse is going to leave, let him or her do the filing. Why? Because if he or she makes the choice to leave, the Scriptures are clear that the remaining, believing spouse is freed for a future. According to 1 Corinthians 7:15, "If the unbeliever departs, let him depart; a brother or a sister is not under bondage in such cases." The meaning of those words is clear: The marriage bonds are biblically described as being dissolved—the believing spouse is "free."

Older Children

There is a vast difference between relating to older children and young children. And in this part of the chapter, I am addressing parents who did not know Christ and thus raise their children wisely or in ways that make this matter far more natural in reference to spiritual things. Also, today, many remarried parents with blended families may have only been together with the children for a short time.

By "older children" I refer more to the response pattern of the child than his or her age. A child of ten or eleven could have become fairly well fixed in his ways. With the nature of today's society, which cultivates independence and fosters rebellion as a virtue, a child does not have to be naturally strong-willed to embrace self-assertiveness. The spirit of our paganizing culture—a mood and atmosphere spreading like a spiritual cloud breathed by the

husband. Threats, not to mention actual physical beating, are never acceptable, and the Bible's call to marital fidelity and the effort to sustain a marriage in a spirit of sacrificial love does not require yielding to painful or psychologically brutal treatment.

Prince of Darkness—is fostering an adamant posture in the hearts of many youth by seeking to establish their resistance of God.

In the wake of this darkness, God's Word gives us two wonderful promises for older children. Isaiah 54:13 speaks to parents whose children once walked with the Lord: "All your children shall be taught by the LORD, and great shall be the peace of your children." That wonderful promise links our responsible teaching to its fulfillment. Such teaching refers to:

- a model that shows *understanding* as you show the way;
- a listening ear to the *interests* of the child;
- clear expectations—i.e., rules that make sense and are always *consistent* in administration;
- gracious and *trust-building* behavior removing from the child any lifestyle that would reveal hypocrisy or double-mindedness; and
- a *firm* but gentle hand on the child's life, with a *clear-headed* logic attending *explanations* of issues or concerns, but not with chest-thumping authority or ranting criticism.

Jeremiah 31:15–17 is the second promise, which we explained earlier. It offers hope when "taught" kids have wandered and seem beyond a manageable aligning at the moment. All your children "shall come back to their own border"—away from the land of the enemy. These passages afford rich promises to those who want to see their children growing in healthy, sound-minded ways that embrace the

Lord and His ways as well. There are two guidelines that I would suggest.

First, never push or goad children out of fear that if you do not do so, nothing will happen. If they are resistant, pushing only increases resistance. The human response to "push" is "push back."

Let's take an example. Do you want your older child to go to church with you? As long as she lives in your house, then there are gracious ways to require her to go to church or do anything else the family is doing. Guide her gently with a combination of love and authority. In this case simply say, "This is what we do. We go to church as a family. I'm not requiring you to do anything else but to be there." If children are in a healthy church atmosphere, where other kids obviously love Jesus and have their heads on straight, it will become irresistible and that kid will open her heart to the Lord. A stance of dominance will not help a parent make headway; an inviting and lovingly provoking stance will.

As a general rule, if you have had a believing home, even with imperfections, and your child just wants to "do her own thing," then for the time being I think you have every reason—even responsibility—to say, "This is what our family does." With the right approach you give evidence of the family as a unit irrespective of the culture's effort to invade, and by drawing a child into the love-web of a family with purpose you can sustain the older child's involvement with you.

There are many not-so-simple illustrations, of course. Suppose you and your spouse have just recently received the Lord, and you have a seventeen-year-old son who is on drugs or hanging out with the wrong crowd or dealing with some other major problem. You are probably not going to get too far by saying that as long as he is living in your house, he is going to church. That problem was bred in another context and is going to have to be resolved in another way. Use wisdom.

The second guideline for older children is this: Recognize rebellion for what it is. Rebellion is a spirit. It is demonic at its root. The Bible equates rebellion with "the sin of witchcraft" in a biblical context that unveils both rebellion and demonism as a quick path to personal ruin (see 1 Samuel 15:23).

This is not at all to say that a child who is in rebellion is demon-possessed. It means that he or she has consciously made choices—whether in relative innocence or with pointed willfulness. Through choices of the child's own will, the "soul turf" became exposed and "place" was made for the adversary. He never misses a chance to assign his cohorts a mission to take up "squatter's rights" if the territory is vacant.

Hosts of Christian parents are either ignorant of or fearful of coming to understand behavior patterns that suggest either the subtleties or ferocity of demonic influence. But we have the truth of God's Word that not only empowers us against the devil but also assures us that we have no reason to fear. "God has not given us a spirit of fear, but of power and of love and of a sound mind" (2 Timothy 1:7). And it is healthy to *personalize* 1 John 4:4, paraphrasing its truth and declaring aloud: *"Jesus Christ my Savior-King is the 'One Greater' than my adversary the devil."* In His name we are "more than conquerors," and as Isaiah 54:17 says, "No weapon formed against you shall prosper."

What does this mean in relation to a rebellious child? It means that the Lord has given you authority over that spirit.

Begin to take a position against it and do battle in prayer. You win this type of battle in the realm of prayer, not in the things you say and do with the child. Bad behavior needs to be confronted, but our primary parental prayer mission is this: *In faith and with passion, you need to raise an invisible, God-enforced wall of divine protection—a shield of defense— around your home.* Daily prayer and discerning sensitivity that refuse any space—any turf—to be intruded upon by the darkness are available. As surely as sniveling spirits are slithering to position themselves for entry, ask the Father to commission His angels to patrol the boundary of your dwelling and to monitor any activity of the enemy. "The name of the LORD is a strong tower; the righteous run to it and are safe" (Proverbs 18:10). Hallelujah!

Younger Children

Ministering to younger children is easier because they are not as fixed in their behavior patterns and thought processes. The problem for Christian parents, though, is that many of them become anxious about securing their children's salvation, and, as a result, some children say they have received Jesus before they understand enough to truly yield to Him. As much as parents would like to lead their children to the Lord, without the ministry of the Holy Spirit nobody can say Jesus is Lord.

Not only are some parents anxious to have their children come to the Lord, but they want to be the ones to lead them there. They press at every opportunity. We can pressure kids to say they have asked Jesus into their hearts. We can get them baptized in water, even lead them to an experience of being baptized with the Holy Spirit. But if we do not allow the natural rise of the crop of Kingdom life, we are force-feeding the growth of the tree instead of just planting the seed and letting it grow in a healthy and appropriate way.

Parents who push too hard too early can end up with kids who have knowledge of spiritual facts, but not an understanding of spiritual things. To avoid this, allow God's work in the child's heart to grow like the seed Jesus described; hear His teaching about how the Kingdom comes into and develops in a life. He said that the Kingdom comes like this: "The earth yields crops by itself: first the blade, then the head, after that the full grain in the head" (Mark 4:28). His practical picture is as beautiful in its promise as it is realistic in its time-expectation. It teaches us to avoid wanting the full-orbed grain in the head of the wheat shock before it is time for harvest. It's a date we should not try to push, but it is a time we dare not miss.

In 1 Samuel 3, the Bible tells the story of the child Samuel who ministered to the Lord under Eli, the high priest. This idea of trusting the Holy Spirit to do the work while we pray is exemplified beautifully by Eli's guidance of the young lad. One night Samuel returned to Eli's bedside three times asking if the priest had called him. When Eli perceived how God was dealing with the child, he gave simple counsel as to how to respond when God speaks. Then he offered sensible follow-through after the boy heard God's voice. We will see the evidence of this imprinting on young Samuel's life in chapter 11, which discusses his life and ministry in more detail.

It really is exciting to watch the grace of God moving in a child's life. The Lord is so creative. As unique and special as children are, so unique and special are God's dealings with them. The Lord will give you sensitivity to that. When you perceive that the Lord is doing something with a child, you don't need to spring on it and come through with a big message. It is sometimes as though a blade comes up through the ground and we want to pound a two-by-four beside it to help support it.

Jesus, in Matthew 19:14, said, "Suffer little children, and forbid them not, to come unto me" (KJV). I used to think He was saying, "Don't keep the children from coming to Me," but I think it has a slightly different focus. The word *suffer* means "to allow or permit." Jesus was saying that we are to let them come to Him naturally, not push them into Him.

Children are great inquirers. Be sensitive. Allow them to come. Demonstrate faith. Be prepared to answer when they ask. Never crowd them. Trust God. And receive the beauty of His harvest as He gives it.

Relatives

Proverbs 18:24 says something that a lot of people probably never think of when it comes to bringing people to Jesus. It says: "A man who has friends must himself be friendly, but there is a friend who sticks closer than a brother." If you want to win people, be winsome.

In Luke 15:1–2 the Bible says that Jesus was at dinner with a group of people who were forthrightly and publicly labeled by the Pharisees as "sinners." His presence in no way compromised His own values, but His tactic was to let them feel His acceptance of them as *people*. Blackballing the lost, personally or corporately as a congregation, by attitude or public rejection, is not Jesus' style. We are called to welcome people with all graciousness, even though they may offend the standards we would expect of any true believer and we would require of any membership applicant.

Jesus' model is clearly there to make the point. We need to learn how to maintain our character while reaching out to the lost, but there are many we will never touch—including relatives and friends—without identifying with them or taking time intentionally to develop friendships with them.

Earlier I told the story of hoping to gain an entry point in reaching one of my relatives, first by indicating my care for him as a person and thus hoping he would realize God's care for his soul. And while you will remember I blindly developed hardness of heart toward him and failed to pray until God revealed it to me, I did, however, do one thing right. I invited him to go bowling as a friend and relative knowing not only that he excelled at the sport but that as a child he had been taught that "bowling is sin"; doubtless that was one of many other unbiblical, legalistic rules he was taught and that surely contributed to his rebellion.

We have no idea how many loved ones or others we are trying to reach who are rebelling against a "God" who does not exist—if you base their concept of Him on supposed demands that are other than benevolent. Study the Bible: Even God's *real* prohibitions are for our good.

The greatest tool of evangelism when it comes to loved ones is to be genuinely loving and friendly to them without the taint of manipulation. Consider some of the "well-meaning" things that people will do. A gal visits her folks in Omaha for a week and leaves the bed all nicely made up. But when her mom pulls back the bedspread, she finds a couple of tracts left there. For

71

Christmas, this daughter sends her parents Christian books and CDs. She never fails to say, "Praise the Lord!" She plans a weekend visit around a business trip, but says, "I'm going to church tomorrow," hoping to impress them, even though they only have a day and a half together.

Does she really think they will want to get saved when she returns from church? Those things are absolutely counterproductive. What will make a difference is that relatives see the quality in your life. Wait to talk about it until they ask you to tell them.

By the way, you should not presume that you will be the instrument by which your family comes to the Lord. And don't pout if you are not! We are the ones to love, we are the ones to pray, we are the ones to insert the leaven and let the yeast take over from there. Plant the seed and let it grow. Be a friend. Let the love of God show.

Principles in Our Witness

Here, then, are four principles to keep in mind as we endeavor to plant that tiny mustard seed:

1. *Remember that we are locked in spiritual warfare for these souls.* Fiery darts of the enemy are going to be flung, and sometimes feelings will get hurt in the process. The enemy seeks to drive a wedge between you and your loved ones, hoping that you will lose your heart of compassion for them.

Concept: Don't react to human beings when your real adversary is the cause of your frustration.

2. *Ask God for wisdom in your conduct toward them.* We do not want to live under legalism and bondage. We need wisdom so that we know how to relate to those we love (see James 1:5). Avoid prudishness and being concerned about appearances. There are some good guidelines in Romans 14:14–22. Be careful not to be typecast as the family religious weirdo (see Colossians 4:4–6).

Concept: Holiness is more a "heart" than a "rule" issue. Guard your heart and don't spank people with your rules.

3. *Let your speech be appropriate to the situation.* We should not enter into communication in which the good things we say will only be mocked. Jesus warned against casting your pearls before swine (see Matthew 7:6). He was not saying that human beings are pigs. He was saying that when people do not appreciate the precious thing you have to offer, they will wallow in what services their own appetites. If people are not going to be responsive to you, don't bother to communicate something that is going to create a setting for mockery. Be sensitive for the right timing. Ask the Holy Spirit to give you grace and wisdom, and let your presence communicate that to others.

Concept: Your tongue should be a delivery of "salt" (Colossians 4:6); its purpose is not to sting the infection of sin in people, but to bring healthy, desirable flavor as a result of your presence.

4. *Be sensitive and sensible.* Show interest in the members of your family. Do they think you care about them as

73

persons, or only as souls to be saved? Yes, they are spiritual beings, but they also have thoughts and feelings and physical needs. If you love and care about them as people, you will be planting the good seed in the ground or working the leaven into the dough. And Jesus promises that when we do that very, very little thing that we need to do, and do it with the right heart, supporting it with prayer, then the Kingdom will enter and eventually complete the good work.

Concluding Concept: Winning people to Christ is not conquering them or verifying yourself. It is about showing so much of Jesus that they cannot resist Him.

7

HEIRS TOGETHER
OF THE GRACE OF LIFE

Wives . . . husbands . . . being heirs together of the grace
of life.

1 Peter 3:1, 7

We began this book with my describing the Holy Spirit's
call to rise in prayer and resist a warlike assault—
one launched by Satan against unity among believers and
against the health of homes, cities and nations. This attack
is nowhere more apparent than his broad-scale assault on
believing homes—instances where only one family member
is a believer as well as instances where mutual faith exists
throughout the home.

All hell understands the powerful dynamic that is available through the "lighthouse" of a believing home and the beauty of a healthy marriage that honors Christ. If you are a married Christian couple, please know that you are a primary and unique target of the adversary's assault. To some degree, I believe this is true because of the biblical revelation that a unique endowment of the Holy Spirit is available to you as a pair of believers, united.

It would seem there is an awesome invitation to power for the prayer life of a banded-for-prayer married couple. Since Christ said, "If two of you agree on earth concerning anything that they ask, it will be done for them by My Father in heaven" (Matthew 18:19), consider the "ready agreement" potential of a couple growing in partnership, knowing and living and exercising the "grace" of being "heirs together." It bodes promise and potential unlike anything else in our world. But it needs to be built upon the foundation of a *growing* relationship between husband and wife. Their union is crucial for the release of the distinct inheritance God offers them. Let's look into how a couple can learn and apply this dynamic most effectively.

A New Identity

As God develops a husband and wife's relationship, they begin to exist as a new identity—the one He designed them to become when the two were joined. There is no counterpart to it in all of creation. When the Bible says that the two "shall become one flesh" (Genesis 2:24; see also Matthew 19:5; Mark 10:8; Ephesians 5:31), it is saying much more about their union than a sexual partnership.

The two become *another entity*, and the sum is greater than its parts.

As a two-become-one, grace-formed entity, every couple is designed by God to experience a dimension of dominion that is especially given to them. It goes back to God's creative order. When He made humankind, He decreed three aspects of inheritance for husbands and wives: that they would (1) be fruitful, (2) multiply and (3) have dominion (see Genesis 1:28). While the habit of most readers of Genesis 1 is to treat those phrases as romantic poetry, God's Word is speaking rich substance in three realms: vocation, procreation and administrative partnership with God.

1. God wants each person to be effective, productive and fulfilled in the stewardship of his or her gifting. For the first couple, the Garden was not only a beautiful place but also a rich base of agricultural productivity: "Replenish the earth and subdue it," God said.

2. The obvious intent of childbearing and rearing was a call given them, and the God who invented our sexual passions was unquestionably calling husbands and wives to ever-deepening intercommunication and mutuality of respect, fulfillment and ecstasy as well.

3. The call to "dominion" (Hebrew *rawdad*) means essentially to subjugate or rule over, to beat down. God was indicating a call to steward spiritual authority, knowing that their domain would come under attack. Had they kept "teamed as one," each one shielding the other, it is dubious the serpent would have succeeded.

If you are married, there is a dimension of dominion waiting to be exercised in areas of life that you touch in a way that nobody else touches. It starts with the privilege of literally partnering with God in the creation of a new life. The Creator's intention for marriage and family as He ordained begins in this way and, though violated by people in the millions annually, is recoverable as a life value every time a believing marriage is sealed. As parents, the power of agreeing in prayer and both blessing and shielding your children is a beginning point. As believers, think of this: If God can use your partnership to bring about human birth, He offers "grace" in life-giving as you pray together for people to be born again!

Being heirs together means that a husband has been given clear responsibilities: (1) to be devoted to his wife's interests and well-being; (2) to be tenderly sensitive to her in every way; (3) to lead the way in seeking the above referenced possibilities of their union.

Equally true, the wife is accountable to God as well: (1) to love and respect her husband; (2) to encourage his leadership, not as denial of her gifts or intelligence, but as an act of faith that God will bless their marriage as a true partnership where neither is "boss," but each is contributing to the team; (3) to lead the way in making their home a place of peace—a healthy environment for their teaming to train and raise their kids.

A Wider Scope

The scope of your joint-inheritance may broaden as you "tend the turf" around you—prayerfully having impact on your neighborhood, business, nation and world. In both great need and large issues, the Bible gives reference to couples uniting to fast and pray in mutual agreement (see 1 Corinthians 7). Weigh wisely the fact that the Word of God teaches prayer with fasting as a profoundly dynamic means of breaking through satanically structured spiritual obstacles at multiple dimensions related to practical daily life as well as national and international strife.

This brief summary holds miracle potential. It is worth the time it takes to build a marriage relationship that discovers and grows in spiritual partnership as well as domestic and romantic coupling. It is yours to build on the foundation of God's Word and way. Make up your minds: If you accept the terms you will gain the joy and the triumphs of your grace-given and unique inheritance as heirs together.

8

YOUR PRAYERS
ARE DECISIVE!

Therefore I exhort first of all that supplications, prayers, intercessions, and giving of thanks be made for all men, for kings and all who are in authority, that we may lead a quiet and peaceable life in all godliness and reverence. For this is good and acceptable in the sight of God our Savior, who desires all men to be saved and to come to the knowledge of the truth. For there is one God and one Mediator between God and men, the Man Christ Jesus.

1 Timothy 2:1–5

One Christmas season not long ago, in the midst of the happy rain of cards that came to our house with notes of greetings and testimonies that are so delightful to read, there was a letter from a gentleman living in the Hawaiian Islands who had been a part of our congregation in the past. He mentioned having seen our telecast during which we had declared ourselves in a stance against drug trafficking. While these regular prayer gatherings were not televised, a broadcast had invited viewers to join our "Prayer Warfare."

The decision to engage in this "war" took place as a result of one of our ministry teams leading the congregation to join the President's "War on Drugs." We realized that both the least and the greatest things we could do were to pray and to continue earnestly for a season. For example, we asked the Lord to bring to light "the hidden things of darkness" as we launched a prayer advance against the evil—men and demons—controlling the drug cartel as well as the street drug peddlers. We invoked a penetration of God's unveiling and exposing work, praying specifically that enforcement personnel would be able to break in and overthrow organized traffickers, and that God's power would break through to block the horrific, continual spread of human bondage to drugs.

Understanding that we wrestle not against flesh and blood but against spiritual hosts of wickedness, we began as a congregation to wrestle in prayer—that is, to pray with concerted passion—that we might see the overthrow of those works of hell that manifest themselves in that way. It was our response to our national leader's call to warfare. It was not the first time over the decades that a Spirit-motivated compulsion to pray, one part of a pattern of continuing intercession, had been a focus of our Wednesday night prayer meeting.

Long ago, we had received a word of prophecy calling us to intercessory accountability, irrespective of what any other group did. God told us that if we would take our stance in prayer, He would move in power. So this was not a matter of considering our prayers to be more righteous or less righteous than others' prayers; rather, our obedience held the promise of decisive answers if we would receive and obey His assignment.

Thus, I was particularly interested in the news the Hawaiian gentleman delivered. He described how moved he was to discover that within two weeks of the start of our prayer campaign he read a notice in a Honolulu newspaper that the largest drug bust in history—anywhere—had just occurred here in Los Angeles. Agents had discovered a shipment coming from Colombia. This person wrote: "It so excited me that no sooner had you launched the warfare than there came that encouraging signal of God answering your prayers."

When I read that, I felt embarrassed. Not because God had moved in response to the many prayers being offered, but because I had not made the connection. I think it was the first of many multimillion-dollar drug busts, and I had not associated it with our having entered prayer two weeks before it took place. It served to remind me again of two things, and to review them with my flock.

First, prayer is often *immediately effective.*

When we pray, decisive things *do* happen. But just as my friend had to write me from 2,500 miles away to let me know, I urge you to ponder the fact that God is at work beyond our sight and sound. Don't doubt it. Sometimes He may not let us know what He is doing because of our excitement over Step One when we still have Steps Two through Nine to go!

Remember, the interlacing of human circumstance is complex. Some things we ask God to do for someone we love may be linked to other lives in which God is also at work; there may be other processes He is engaging to bring about the ultimate answer for which we pray.

Our part again is basic: When you pray, believe and hold the matter before God with thanksgiving after that (see Philippians 4:6–7). His part is to penetrate the grid of circumstances of all lives involved as He wills to release His blessing and salvation, grace and power, and answer the request you have made.

I am not suggesting this is always the reason for delays, but we need to remember that when we pray, "Yours is the Kingdom and the power and the glory," we are not making a recitation—it is a proclamation. "Lord, I'm surrendering the timing to You and letting You drive the bus. I may not know the stops You need to make, but I am going to sit here and praise You until we reach the place where my answer steps on board!"

Second, *no request* is too big.

Perhaps along with those in your particular family whom you pray for, you feel love and compassion being awakened for those beyond your touch—for the wounded and hurting in the world, for those who are carrying a burden of helplessness, especially who neither understand how to pray nor even know they can. The question rises: Am I overreaching my prayer privileges? Am I presuming to pray too broadly or concerning a matter too large for my faith?

Maybe a specific cause stirs your heart—medical advances for an illness that has touched your family, missionaries working with a particular people group, or a nation's turmoil where tribal hatred or hunger seems relentless. There are innumerable arenas of opportunity for plain believers like you and me to engage in great issues in prayer.

Years ago I invited all the members of our congregation to ask the Holy Spirit to impress upon their hearts the name of a nation beyond our own that He would assign them to pray for. As a result, Anna began to pray for a beleaguered eastern European nation while I was moved to pray for a Saharan country rarely referred to in the news—its low population and deserted landmass made it rather a non-entity in popular terms.

But once we each began to pray, amazing things began to happen, giving us encouragement about our prayers. Foremost, it seemed we began noting news items, reading magazine articles and hearing passing reports of happenings in the two countries we were praying for. Some may wonder if that information was equally available before. I don't know; maybe it was. But that is not the point. The point is that it seems to me that when you and I begin to bring matters to God at His throne, He is going to share matters with us where we are! Today, especially via the Internet, it is amazing to consider the prayer partnerships we can form—networking with other people the Holy Spirit is calling to pray regarding almost any issue or nation.

This is a good thing, because God invites us to "come boldly to [His] throne of grace" (Hebrews 4:16)! It is as though the Lord of heaven is saying, "Bring it on," urging us to come regarding "big things" in the same Spirit of faith He breathed upon the early Church. I was inspired to write a song some years ago that expresses God's heart in this vein.

It's a small thing to ask God to do a great thing;
And it's a great thing to ask God to do a small thing.
So do not fear to pray—open your heart and say,
"Father I come today, to ask a great thing" or "a
small thing."
It's a small thing for God to do a great thing;
Call unto Him, He'll work beyond your imagining.
Little or large the need, simply come and believe—
Bring to Him all things—
Your great or small things.
Our Father's will is clear, "Ask anything!"
So now pray in Jesus' Name,
For there's nothing too hard for God.

Jack W. Hayford

Great prayer does not require greatly recognized people. This couplet was penned over a century ago:

Satan trembles when he sees
The weakest saint upon his knees!

It reminds us pointedly never to surrender to either hopelessness or helplessness in the face of large issues. The Holy Spirit is *the Helper*, and He is a prayer specialist. Ask Him to enable, energize and enrich your prayer life.

When "bold and believing prayer" is taught, inevitably a few people ask me, "How do I know if I'm praying presumptuously?" When that happens, I ask two things:

1. Are you asking for something selfish or stupid? Answer: "Well, no."
2. Do you fear you might pray for something opposed to God's will? Very often the answer will be, "Yes."

In responding to this common fear or uncertainty, I show people 1 John 5:14: "Now this is the confidence that we have in Him, that if we ask anything according to His will, He hears us." Then I explain the following.

God has not invited us to discern His will when we pray; He has taught us to pray, "Your Kingdom come, *Your will be done.*" This being true, the words in 1 John are saying, "You have the privilege of coming with confidence, for the Father has called you to pray, *asking anything,* and *that* is what His will is. He wills *that* we pray, and we can rest in the confidence that He knows best and will act accordingly, while being comforted with the fact that He also rejoices in our obedience: We prayed!

Please understand, dear reader: I am not just pointing this out to answer interesting questions. I want to reach out and take your hand and encourage you to believe that your prayers are being called forth by the heart of God and your prayers will be decisive.

Think about this. There are people all over the world who are crying out right now in their personal moments of desperation—crying in a thousand languages as you read this word, speaking their own heart-cry that translates, "Oh, God, help me!" God hears everyone, and also wants us to circle His throne as a mammoth prayer band—each one likely alone in a room at his or her devotions. He is saying, "Take the hand of the lonely, sick or broken you have never met, those who would not understand, and even some who don't understand My Son's life or love or truly understand the truth about Me. But I love them. And your partnership with them and Me, as you pray 'in Jesus' name,' or as you pray in the Spirit beyond your own understanding, will become effective—will be decisive."

Do not suppose that the cries of lost souls in their crises are not heard by God. While salvation alone comes through Jesus, His Son, the mercies of God come to people whatever their understanding of or ignorance about Him, whatever their just or unjust ways of life (see Matthew 5:45).

When desperate hearts cry, God hears—and His desire is to answer prayers, even from people like you and me who do not deserve a thing, for His mercy endures forever!

Prayer is the choice we make where we want the rule of God to come. And when we see things out of order, outside His rule, whether in our families, neighborhoods, churches or cities, we can pray decisive prayers and He will come.

The Lord is looking for people who will take His Word and apply it to the matters the Holy Spirit directs them to intercede for, and those situations that we may not understand, but feel the prompting of God's heartbeat to pray about.

Such prayer does not require a feeling to be a prayer of faith. Faith is not a feeling; faith is an action. Faith is obeying God's rule. When He says to "ask anything" or when you are moved to pray for a certain thing, do it. The fruit will be harvested later. You will sense the pleasure of God that you prayed, even if you know neither the circumstance nor the answer until we step inside the doors of heaven. And the result—we can be sure—will *always* be for His glory!

9

Upon Your Sons and Daughters

And it shall come to pass in the last days, says God, that I will pour out My Spirit on all flesh; your sons and your daughters shall prophecy, your young men shall see visions, your old men shall dream dreams. And on My menservants and on My maidservants I will pour out My Spirit in those days; and they shall prophecy.

Acts 2:17–18

It was about four o' clock in the morning and I was awakened, not by a prompting of the Lord, but by the fact I was in Manila, and my body had not adjusted yet to my other-side-of-the-world time zone. I didn't want to get up—I needed to sleep—so as I lay there in the darkened room, I said, "Lord, if

You will, tell me what You want me to pray for." His strong but gentle voice immediately impressed this upon my spirit: *Pray for an outpouring of the Holy Spirit on your children.*

What occurred that morning has become a way of life today, but at that moment I simply named each child and grandchild and spoke that blessing over them. At that time, Anna and I had a grand total of sixteen: four children (eight including their spouses) and eight grandchildren. Today, including Anna and me, our clan totals 32! It makes a great celebration in itself at either Christmas or Thanksgiving!

Upon returning to Los Angeles after ministering to the conference of Filipino pastors I was addressing at the National Convention Center, I felt constrained to broaden the message of this "word"—being particularly stirred by the prophecy of Joel 2. My sense of urgency was born of the fact that this is a "last days" prophecy, and was also the prophetic text recalled to verify God's fresh, new outpouring of the Spirit on the day the Church was born: "It shall come to pass in the last days, says God, that I will pour out of My Spirit on all flesh; your sons and your daughters shall prophesy, your young men shall see visions" (Acts 2:17).

I also realized that God had moved at our church in such a way as to grow and send many young couples from our doors into ministry across America and around the world. Often I will "pray the map"—asking God to "pour out Your Spirit upon young leaders," and ask Him to dispense "latter rains of blessing" on those in that region, sometimes naming every state in the United States, and moving on throughout the world's continents as well. (I have worked at learning the names of most countries in the world so I can "visually travel" each continent and reach the hands of my heart toward it as I pray.)

To this day, Anna and I pray for God's outpouring of His Spirit on our kids several times a day, each of us being prompted when we see a specific time (during any hour) on a digital clock. My sense is this: The deeper we move into the last days, the greater the need for our young people to have the shelter and the shield, the presence and the power, the wisdom and discernment of the Holy Spirit!

Overcoming the Darkness

As we ask the Father to answer this prayer, it is important to clarify our target. We are not parroting a ritual phrase, but taking its theme to broaden and deepen our focus as we move into specifics. For instance, in what ways might we ask for an outpouring?

We need a great upheaval—a shaking and shaping of a generation of young people. They are being ground to dust by our culture, for they are growing up in a world that is polluted beyond measure. However disturbed your background or mine may have been, few of us experienced anything of the dimensional darkness of today's mindless, pointless environment of hopelessness and confusion surrounding our children.

I am not hanging a funereal crepe of despair. It is simply a matter of looking at the realities of our culture and recognizing what it is doing to our kids. The spirit of darkness that is being poured out upon them can only be "washed away" by an outpouring of the Holy Spirit. Only He can neutralize what is accumulating as the adversary vents his fury in his last-ditch effort to capture millions. Revelation 12:12 says, "The devil has come down to you, having great wrath, because he knows that he has a short time." This provides a context that dramatically designates the adversary we face, the time we live in and the call to battle. How trumpet-like a summons to hear the words: *Pray for an outpouring of the Spirit on your children!*

Ammunition for the Battle

Looking at the force and ferocity of the adversary's intent and fury, and viewing what ground he has already gained with this generation, we need to feed on God's promises if we are going to join others who will first pray for their own children and move into intercession for those kids' generation. The promises are ammunition for the battle; they are assurances we are not merely breathing words into the sky or living in a dream world and jousting with windmills. Consider these promising texts for starters.

Under a similar call and at a pivotal historic moment, Jeremiah the prophet spoke to the people in a city that was dying in the sewage and filth of its own corruption, but God promised hope.

> For I know the thoughts that I think toward you, says the LORD, thoughts of peace and not of evil, to give you a future and a hope. Then you will call upon Me and go and pray to Me, and I will listen to you. And you will seek Me and find Me, when you search for Me with all your heart. I will be found by you, says the LORD, . . . and I will bring you to the place from which I cause you to be carried away captive.
>
> Jeremiah 29:11–14

Please notice the relationship between the promise of the future and the place of prayer. Prayer is pivotal to appropriate God's promise.

- "You will seek Me and find Me." When? "When you search for Me with all your heart."
- What will happen then? "I will be found by you and I will bring you back from your captivity."

It is not redundant to look again at another of Jeremiah's prophecies, the words in chapter 31 about weeping for lost children, which we studied together earlier. Read again how Jeremiah gave God's command, essentially saying, "Don't waste your tears." It is our reminder never to be dismayed however dark the horizon. God is calling us to pray, and receive a rising of "the Sun of Righteousness . . . with healing in His wings" (Malachi 4:2). Whatever anguish tempts doubt, hear the word of the Lord:

> Thus says the Lord: "A voice was heard in Ramah, lamentation and bitter weeping, Rachel weeping for her children, refusing to be comforted for her children, because they are no more."
>
> [However, in the face of anguish of the moment the command is issued.]
>
> Thus says the Lord: "Refrain your voice from weeping, and your eyes from tears; for your work shall be rewarded, says the Lord, and they shall come back from the land of the enemy. There is hope in your future, says the Lord, that your children shall come back to their own border."
>
> Jeremiah 31:15–17

Only one word rises to my lips as I write those words again: "Wow!" What a certainty. What an impending victory. What a mighty deliverer our God is!

Do you ache for a child who is lost? Perhaps she is physically removed? Perhaps he is emotionally distant? The Lord says, "Your children will return to their own boundaries—their own borders. No matter where they have drifted or whatever problem engulfs them, *pray for an outpouring of the Spirit upon your own and this generation's children* and I will pour out My Spirit, and your sons and daughters will speak My word."

These prophetic words provide our mandate if we would receive that outpouring. The pivotal issue is *that* we pray, that we pray in *faith* and that we target actions to accompany our prayers. Let's strategize together.

"That" We Pray

The idea *that* we must pray is obvious because of the crying need of the children and youth around us. This is not just a word for parents. Every adult in every church congregation should be assisted to see the significance of prayer for the young ones in his or her midst. Everyone is in touch with children or their needs by reason of where they work. And reminders to pray are everywhere—children are in everyone's neighborhood; we see kids almost every time we drive a car or go to the grocery store.

At this hour our children are being pressed by evil times. They are oppressed by dark circumstances that are seeking to shape them in the image of an environment of lost values. The literal word for *perilous* used in the Greek text of 2 Timothy 3:1 describes the last days as "evil, ferocious, lion-like and demon-filled." As the forces are pouring out of hell like brands of fire, we can call for an outpouring of heaven to quench them and a river of the Holy Spirit's power to swamp them. Take a look at a scriptural parallel with a dual insight for our grasp.

When Israel was enslaved in Egypt just before her deliverance, the Bible describes a plague of darkness that could be felt (see Exodus 10:21) coming over the land. It is helpful to our purpose and our praying to understand that this was not so much an *invoked* darkness but a *provoked* one. In other words, God's judgment was not descending upon the land with darkness of His begetting; rather, He was withdrawing His hand to reveal to Egypt the full force of the darkness to which Pharaoh's throne was submitting.

It is a sad thing when a nation's sins accumulate to the point that God says, "Here, if you want that, you can have all of it and the hideous things that come with it. You have removed yourself from My mercy and its preventative grace." *Preventative grace* is a term we use to describe the merciful actions of God—essentially unseen in their execution and, by many, seldom honored because God's kindnesses are presumed to be our right (if indeed He does exist, as unbelievers say).

The plague of thick darkness reigned for three days— three days of horror, designed to awaken Pharaoh and his people to the error of their ways, to show them the "benefits" of the idols they served if those demon-gods were unleashed upon them. The fall of a nation as a globe-dominating empire would follow shortly, and all because the wake-up call of disaster brought no leaders—nor the people they led—to repentance. (It is significant to note that each of the plagues represented something thought by the Egyptians to be under the control of one of the "gods" of the nation's pantheon.)

The above explanation is not simply for the sake of our information; it is intended to give rise to our discerning intercession and to lift our hearts with inspiration. I suggest this because the text reporting the thick darkness in Egypt also relays a companion miracle. Read the full passage:

> Then the LORD said to Moses, "Stretch out your hand toward heaven, that there may be darkness over the land of Egypt, darkness which may even be felt." So Moses stretched out his hand toward heaven, and there was thick darkness in all the land of Egypt [for] three days. They did not see one another; nor did anyone rise from his place for three days. But all the children of Israel had light in their dwellings.
>
> verses 21–23

Now, look with me and see the dynamic truths present for our imbibing from this portion of God's Word—and we surely need its emboldening and rejoicing hope. There are two take-away truths here.

First, neither the darkness over Egypt nor the reason for its presence is much different from the social, moral, spiritual and economic cloud over many nations. It is thick and it "can be felt." Further, it is here for the same reason: America, for instance, has invited God *out* of its life, His Word *out* of its educational system and His moral values *out* of its laws. The plagues of venereal disease, gang warfare, teen suicide, divorce (the list could go on) are the direct outflow of the darkness to which our land has surrendered. *However*, our nation has not yet been swamped to the point of complete ruin—and therein is our call. As people who know our God, prayer for our land can bring healing. The passage is a virtual signal flag, summoning us with the assurance that it is not too late yet. God's mercy promises that with our intercession, "Help is on the way!" (see 2 Chronicles 7:14; 1 Timothy 2:1–5).

Second, "all the children of Israel had light in their dwellings." I do not need to write much—you get the point, and it is time for another "Hallelujah!" The word *children* in this text, by the way, was an all-inclusive age-group—meaning all the families—but the implications for our present focus are obvious. If we will put prayer for our children on the front burner, calling for an outpouring of the Holy Spirit upon our children—our own, others we know and those of our land—we have reason to expect a glory-light of God to explode miraculously over the land. *Where God is invited in, the light will shine, no matter how dark it is everywhere else!* And until our nation comes to itself—a hope we need to embrace as intercessors—move beside me in prayer that God's light will shine in homes and families as He grants "His people" the presence of His power. And as that is realized, it will begin to spread through us all to all the land!

"How" We Pray

So then, how shall we pray? Here are four Scriptures that reveal specific expressions of the Holy Spirit's nature, which He will enable us to receive as He stands with us to strengthen us in prayer. He is called the Spirit of hope, of faith, of wisdom and of liberty.

The Spirit of Hope. "Now hope does not disappoint, because the love of God has been poured out in our hearts by the Holy Spirit who was given to us" (Romans 5:5). Ask first for the Holy Spirit of hope. As we call for an outpouring of the Spirit, this is the way He works. And by that flow of love in you, two things will happen: Hope will beget intercession, and it will beget tenderness of touch in the places where you begin to reach out.

The Spirit of Faith. "We have the same spirit of faith . . . knowing that He who raised up the Lord Jesus will also raise us up with Jesus, and will present us with you" (2 Corinthians 4:13–14). The Spirit of faith gives confidence that there is no situation too dead for the resurrection power of the Lord to work in. We have the promise that God will at the very least turn the situation around in the person's life. And who knows what He may do beyond that.

I received a gracious letter of gratitude addressed to our congregation by one of our members who understands this kind of life even in the face of death. Before this young man came to Christ some years ago, he was deeply involved in the homosexual lifestyle. At the writing of this letter he was dying of AIDS, yet his words were full of hope—and it was not superficial hope. He knew that he might be healed, but also felt the "whirlwind" of self-destruction he had brought upon himself was something he faced for having "sown to the wind" of rebellion—since in his childhood he had been taught the ways of the Lord.

The source of his peace was a profound Presence he sensed, and any concern for being healed was somehow dimmed in comparison with that. "I feel the Holy Spirit's comfort, assurance and peace—sometimes with a sweetness I can't describe."

I thought how the sweetness he was experiencing may not be describable in earthly terms, but he had a mother whose sweetness and depth of commitment to her son's salvation could be described in one short phrase: *She had been praying for an outpouring of the Spirit of God on her son!*

His letter was a testimony to how the Spirit of faith gives us confidence that there is no situation too deadly for the power of God's *Presence* to intervene. In the case of this lost-but-now-found son, that Presence brought healing to his soul as the Holy Spirit of faith flowed over *him* in answer to steadfast, effective prayer of his mother.

The Spirit of Wisdom. "Wisdom calls aloud outside. . . . Turn at my rebuke; surely I will pour out my spirit on you; I will make my words known to you" (Proverbs 1:20, 23). This work of the Spirit will help children to learn how to live. Wisdom is not the accumulation of information. We have never had a more educationally and technologically advanced culture anywhere in the world. Nor have we ever had a culture closer to blowing the planet apart with a short fuse.

Mere knowledge is not the answer man needs. Wisdom shows you how to take what you know and make it work. The Spirit's assistance by this means is especially critical for keeping on target without seeming to be "gunning" for the soul of a loved one. He will keep you "in sync" with God's timing and touch, so you neither run ahead of His work with your "works," nor reach *into* what He is doing in a loved one's life before He has brought that one *unto.*

Wisdom is poured out by the Spirit of wisdom. Pray for an outpouring of the Spirit of wisdom on the children: "Lord, show them how to live. Show them how to make choices. Show them how to think." God will do it.

The Spirit of Liberty. "Now the Lord is the Spirit; and where the Spirit of the Lord is, there is liberty" (2 Corinthians 3:17).

The Holy Spirit is a Spirit of freeing and deliverance. He is a Spirit of breakthrough. Actually, if you look at Scripture closely you will find that the Spirit of liberty is the Spirit of the Lord—a term in itself that is not generic, but specific in processing the Kingdom rule, the Lordship of Christ in a life. As we pray, the Holy Spirit will—by His *dealings* and by His progressive work of *deliverance*—awaken the soul of the one for whom we pray, while crowding out deceiving voices of the adversary.

The Lord does not pour out His Spirit on our young people in order to give them the holy heebie-jeebies. Oh, God, take us way beyond the superficial notion that getting filled with the Spirit of God is a thrilling but transient moment! He is calling us to anticipate the glory of His presence and power.

That creates hope. And it is not imaginary—it is tangible, real and ready to be fulfilled by an eternally faithful Father. He wants the whole family at His heaven-side table, and He is welcoming you to join in partnership with Him to see that all of yours are there.

10

COMFORTING ONE
ANOTHER IN PRAYER

Therefore we have been comforted in your comfort. And
we rejoiced exceedingly more for the joy of Titus, because
his spirit has been refreshed by you all.

2 Corinthians 7:13

Here is a key point for us to embrace as we persevere
in prayer for our loved ones: Jesus wants to minister
through *us*. You and me. This is important because there is
an enormous tendency in the Body of Christ to depend on
somebody else to be the avenue through which God works in
power. We do not need a professional substitute. We do not
need to line up and have somebody pray for our needs who
we think has a closer connection with God than we have.

I am not saying that prayer lines and platform prayer ministry are an unworthy or unscriptural approach to prayer. I am saying that it can too easily substitute, then supplant, the desire of Jesus to work through each living member of His Body. *Layman* is not really a concept in God's preferred plan. Leaders *are* necessary. Structures *are* worthy. Maturity *is not* present in every member to serve, counsel or minister in some regards. But still, every believer in Christ has an intended place to grow in the local Body of His Church, and every congregation *must find ways* to cultivate the release of God's giftings of life, skill and ability in each member, as well as equip them through teaching on the essential distinctive of partnering with the Holy Spirit in *His* gift-delivery system. He operates it through even the most ordinary people, so every part of the Body is significant for ministry *to* the Body as well as for service *for* it.

I was moved to discuss these basic New Testament discipleship concepts in this book because of several stories I heard once within a short span of time that showed different aspects of ministry through the Body. They came about as the result of the direct and intentional effort we brought amid our church family to be *people on the way to minister today.*

Fundamental in advancing this intentional, purposeful conviction are our regular "prayer circles," which are a four- to five-minute time in virtually every service when we break into small groups of three or four people and pray for each other's needs. This practice is offered to visitors in ways that are inviting and assuring. The brevity makes these circles durably workable, and their regularity is one of the reasons—obviously with ongoing pastoral teaching and exhortation—they became the fulcrum for leveraging growth in "ministry" in the majority of the congregation.

When we speak of ministry in this way, we mean sharing, praying and inviting the Holy Spirit to be in our midst, to assist with discernment and working via His gifts, which He simply and lovingly distributes through everyday "saints" in the Body of the congregation. I want to share several examples to show how prayer from the Body for the Body brings help and comfort.

Ministry through the Body

The first two of the stories referenced above involved words of knowledge through which the Holy Spirit gave healing and direction.

In the first instance, a man gave a testimony in one of our church services about how Jesus had healed him. He explained that I had given a word of knowledge from the pulpit about a person's physical condition and had stated that Jesus Christ was there to touch that condition right then. The man testified how it became evident in the days that followed that the power of God's grace had healed him.

It was very moving. The Holy Spirit used me to deliver a word of knowledge, and God did a wonderful healing work. It was a quiet and natural work of the Lord. And, actually, that is the way it happens most of the time in our church. We do not make a big deal of these moves of God because there is a tendency for them to become kind of a show and take the focus off trusting the Lord.

In another instance a couple came to me and said, "Pastor Jack, we were visiting the church sometime back, and we were at a point in our lives that felt as though we were being torn in two." In fact, the way they described their torment was very much like Paul's words to the Corinthians: "Our bodies had no rest, but we were troubled on every side. Outside were conflicts, inside were fears" (2 Corinthians 7:5). This couple was dealing with a near devastating difficulty, and they knew that they would have to face it when they got home after the service.

They said, "In the service the time came for people to break into little groups and pray for each other. We had never seen prayer circles like that before, but we were not uncomfortable. In fact, we thought it was delightful. Everyone was so loving. We got to pray for others and they prayed for us. The prayers were so genuine."

When the circle concluded, they sat down. Then a young woman from their circle, who was seated in front of them, turned around in her seat to speak to them. She took hold of their hands together and asked if she could share with them a word that the Lord had given her. They asked her please to do so.

"She gave us," they said, "a word of prophecy that was so pointed and so profound that we realized God was telling us the practical way to approach the situation we needed to face when we got home. There was no way this woman could have known about it. We were hearing words of great comfort and receiving great confidence.

"When we got home, we took the simple guidelines the Holy Spirit had given us in that word and applied them to the situation. It became a remarkable pathway to the full solution of something that had been absolutely tormenting our minds when we went into that service."

The ministry of the Holy Spirit in that service through the Body brought comforting direction to those people.

The third story is of a couple who had attended The Church On The Way for three years. Their marriage was in dire condition during that time, but they were in church virtually every Sunday to worship. They testified how the fellowship of the Body and the teaching of the Word brought healing to their marriage and strength into their lives. Today that couple has returned to the public ministry for which they were equipped but had left out of discouragement.

Here is the fourth instance. Anna and I went out to lunch one day. While there, a handsome man in his late thirties or early forties walked up and introduced himself. He said, "I often attend The Church On The Way, although it's not my home church. I'd like to take a moment, if I could, to tell you something." We encouraged him to do so.

"Five years ago," he said, "my life was a wreck. I was messed up in drugs; my head was fouled up. I had been raised in a Christian home but had drifted far, far away from God. One day I realized I needed to go to church, but I didn't know where to go. Where I worked, someone invited me to The Church On The Way. So I came.

"When I walked in the door, two things were evident. The first thing was that I felt the presence of God and the love of people. Because of the way they related, I knew the love of God was there. But I thought of what my mother would have said about going to church in the condition I was in spiritually. She would have said I didn't have a right to go to church; I should get straightened out with God first. But the way people treated me, I knew God was ready to accept me the way I was, and that He could make a difference.

"When we went into the prayer circles," he told us, "well, I had never done anything like that before. But something happened in that circle. I knew while we were praying in the circle that I was changed. For the first time I believed that God was really hearing me and something was really happening. Within one week, everything about my life had changed. I had come into the service with eight cents in my pocket, almost no gas in my car and my soul emptier than both my pocket and my car. Within a week, I was a changed person.

"What has happened in the last five years? God has made me successful in business. He has brought my life back together. Now I am often invited to go to schools and speak to young people about the dead-end street of getting involved in drugs. I just wanted to share that with you."

You can hardly imagine how my heart was warmed. When I heard him tell that story, coupled with the other stories I heard that same week, I realized how vital it is for us to be comforted in prayer as we beseech God on behalf of those we love. It is more important than we might have realized.

Since I mentioned the concept behind and some stories related to our practice of prayer circles, let me answer one of the most common questions asked about them: "What is the response of visitors?"

For the vast majority, it is very positive, because our people are real, hospitable and non-churchy during "Ministry Time"—the name we use for those few minutes that follow twenty minutes of praise-filled, Christ-exalting worship. The message from God's Word will follow, but only *after* the prayer and ministry time. My experience through the years is this: When I take the pulpit to teach the Word of God, and it has been preceded by praise, worship, and people sensibly and sensitively sharing the love of God in prayer and the gifts of God in ministry, everything is *great*. How?

Hearts are open to the Spirit as the Word is presented. Visitors are attentive, because they have tasted something of the reality of God's presence and love. The Body is hungry for more of God's ways because they have been "exercising." The members are truly that—qualified by Christ's life in them, prepared by pastoral and church-wise teaching, and made functional by the power of the Holy Spirit who has filled them and has been given place to overflow the life, love and grace of Jesus Christ *through* them.

Comforting in Hard Times

I am going to present a group of selected words spoken at different times by the apostle Paul. They reflect his candor, transparency and humanity, and remind us how these qualities are central to "the incarnate Word" being over and over "incarnated" in those who have met Jesus the Lord—the Word of God. They are derived from a time in his life and some letters he wrote, and I believe they will help us see clearly how the quality of "humanness" in a believer is essential to his becoming a comfort to others. Joined to praying faith we must have a comforting hand. Meet the apostle Paul now in the midsection of his ministry years. The texts are Acts 18 and the second Corinthian letter.

The letter called 2 Corinthians is part of a story that actually began seven years earlier, as noted in Acts 18, when Paul went to Corinth and a church was born. He served there as a founding pastor for a year and a half, and the people had suffered misunderstanding and great stress. That is what the two letters to the Corinthians are about. The encouraging opening note for us is that the people being addressed knew the Lord Jesus. In other words, troubles are not reserved only for people outside the Body of Christ: We have needs for learning, care, forgiveness, understanding and a will to submit to God's authority—in His Word and through loving servant-leadership.

That is what makes Second Corinthians so unusual among the library of New Testament books. It is the picture of our humanity. It throbs with emotion. It swings back and forth with tidal waves of problems—and amid it all, we find the heart of the Lord to solve them. The key word in this epistle is *comfort, comfort, comfort*. The God who comforts us in all our troubles, He is called "the God of all comfort" in the opening of this letter—the Lord God Almighty who uses His people to help others understand He is also the Lord God All-Caring.

How did Paul help the Corinthians embrace this comfort? He exhibited four actions.

First, he showed a *transparent heart*. Look at these words: "O Corinthians! We have spoken openly to you, our heart is wide open" (2 Corinthians 6:11). Here is the apostle Paul saying, "I'm not going to hide from you."

Second, he made a *forthright disclosure*. Please listen closely. The man who writes that he is troubled on every side by conflicts and fears is the same man who said, "I can do all things through Christ who strengthens me." It is the same man who said, "In all these things we are more than conquerors through Him who loved us." It is the same man who knew the triumphant life of Jesus Christ. Yet he was not inhibited by the truth of the difficulties. He could be honest.

This forthright disclosure is an important feature in a believer's life. Always, I have found some people in other parts of Jesus' Church who will suggest that if you openly describe your pain, your problem, your difficulty or your struggle, then you are "sowing doubt"—poor-mouthing what God has done for you. They may even assert that forthrightness regarding *facts* you face, if they are challenging, problematic or negative, is certain to neutralize vital *faith*. But this criticism cannot hold up against the evidence in God's Word. An immediate example is right here in our study of Paul's words to the Corinthians about his own life-battle.

In this same book, with simple forthrightness, he says: "I asked God three times for an answer to my problem, and it didn't go away" (see 2 Corinthians 12:8). There is legalism in some quarters that would fault Paul for not praying about that thorn just one time, and then praising God and "confessing" the victory. But that is not what Paul did: "I kept asking and, finally, when nothing changed the Lord spoke to me, saying: 'Paul, *My strength is made perfect in weakness, and My grace will be sufficient for you*'" (see verse 9).

With transparency describing his struggle (for there is no answer *he* can speak to his prayer), with candor that describes physical struggle as a demonic attack, and with humility that acknowledges his own bewilderment, Paul concludes his testimony with another kind of victory. Relating to people as an ordinary person, he explains how he learned dependence on God he would not have found otherwise. This does not mean that God did not deliver him, nor that it was God's will he be buffeted. It means that the Great Shepherd *does* bring all His sheep *through*. It also shows that it is biblical to be honest about your struggles and undefensive about those times when your faith seems unproductive. *Forthright disclosure* is not a violation of the principle of faith. It is not yielding to the shadows of doubt. Rather it is stepping into the light of open partnership in prayer—and *with faith*.

Third, he commended a *comforting congregation*. Look at 2 Corinthians 7. Paul had sent Titus to the Corinthians to deliver a letter. Titus returned with words of encouragement from those Paul sought to encourage. In verses 6–7 Paul wrote:

> God, who comforts the downcast, comforted us by the coming of Titus, and not only by his coming, but also by the consolation with which he was comforted in you, when he told us of your earnest desire, your mourning, your zeal for me, so that I rejoiced even more.

He was saying, "I was refreshed because of you, because of your prayer, because of your care for me."

Fourth, he revealed that he was an *affirming believer*. He had formerly been the Corinthians' pastor. He let them know that when he had sent Titus with the letter he had told him, "Titus, whatever the problems may be, those are great people. They know God, and they will stand firm." And when Titus came back he told Paul, "It was just as you said. They loved me. They received me. I was tremendously comforted by them. I came to encourage them; they encouraged me." The power of affirming people, whatever challenges they face, is biblically evidenced and humanly helpful. Moreover, it releases a spirit of mutuality in Christ: Paul says to them, "I had boasted about you to Titus because I knew what you were like, and it made me happy to find out you are still that way" (see 2 Corinthians 7:13–14).

A Pattern to Follow

The beauty of this teaching is that it gives us a pattern we can apply to our own situations. We can find in these words the prayer that comforts. It is a pattern that we can remember and function in always as we pray for our loved ones.

These four guidelines can be used when you join with others in prayer in any format—such as "formally" in a church service prayer circle or meeting casually with friends.

- *Always open your heart honestly.* Paul said, "Our heart is wide open." The man who stood by our table that day said, "Anyone in that circle would have known that my situation wasn't that great. Anybody with any spiritual sensitivity would have known I wasn't walking with God."

- *Always be comforting—not preachy.* The key word is *comfort*—Greek, *paraklesis*—and it means to come alongside because you are invited. When we join others in prayer we are offering to help bear one another's burdens (see Galatians 6:2).

- There are 23 verbs in the New Testament Scriptures that describe how Christians ought to act toward one another—such as edify one another, comfort one another, exhort one another, wait for one another. In other words, come alongside; don't come *at*. Christians who come *at*

111

a person who has a need often make it difficult for that person to receive. "Brother, what you need is more faith. I'm going to pray for you." Do you hear something in the tone of voice? This error comes from trying to mirror in our private experiences and relationships what we see from the platforms in Christendom. A platform is a place for speaking to a group of people so the teacher can be visible. But in our daily lives, we are called alongside people. Identifying with them. Talking with them.

- Be comforting, not preachy, even if you have a strong word that God wants to speak through you. Be patient. Say something like: "Listen, I think the Lord is telling me something for you. Is it okay if I share it with you?" Forget the shaking finger in the air and the deeply intoned "*Gahwd-da* (translated, "God") has a word for you!" Some people may be impressed by that, but other people are going to be scared spitless.

- This reminds me of Dr. Robert Frost, a great Bible teacher now in the presence of the Lord. Dr. Frost said a person once promised him, "If you get the Holy Ghost in your life, He'll put a tiger in your tank." Dr. Frost was a brilliant, learned former professor, a quiet and retiring kind of man; and upon hearing this, prayed, "Lord, I don't want a tiger in my tank. Don't You have something for us bunny rabbits?" Point: God is not a one-size-fits-all in the way He deals with His kids. Each of us may be real, passionate and caring as we share with others, but rather than "being myself," the end outcome through my touch with others needs to "be Jesus."

- The third point is *always pray in faith in Jesus' name*. Invoke Jesus' name. Prayer gatherings are not humanistic

therapy sessions; they are Holy Spirit comfort and healing groups. Granted, there is value in various group en-
terprises; for example, a wide variety of recovery groups
are included in our congregation's ministry—and to
some they bring comfort. But these gatherings are "in
the name of Jesus." We are not there hoping simply to
help people feel better. Our ministry is always target-
ing transformation, by the power of God's Word and
Spirit. The point here is that when we come together to
pray, the resource of power comes not from the milk of
human kindness but from the presence and power of
Jesus' name. Remember with confidence that He said,
"If you ask anything in My name, I will do it."

- *Always be open to the Holy Spirit to give.* The Holy Spirit
  is ready to give gifts. This does not mean that there will
  be a manifestation of a spiritual gift every time you join
  others in prayer. Having said that, I think there are times
  Holy Spirit gifts are delivered through sensitive prayer
  and ministry, and no one particularly recognizes it. The
  test of our effectiveness is not in verifying to ourselves
  that we "did supernatural stuff." Rather, it is that the
  end result is that Jesus Christ is glorified and the Holy
  Spirit is given room to work. Thus, no one need ever
  make a show of functioning in the gifts of the Spirit,
  but we should desire them to be regularly operative and
  functionally present (see 1 Corinthians 14:1)—a word
  of encouragement . . . a word of wisdom . . . a word of
  knowledge . . . a gift of healing. Whatever is needed and
  whatever is appropriate to the moment. In the most
  beautiful way, great things happen when God's great
  Spirit is given place—to give gifts.

Jesus said, "My peace I give unto you, My love I give unto you, My joy I give unto you." When we pray with others He gives His peace, engages the gifts of the Spirit for our use and comforts us in the process. Let's learn now how to live in this place of prayer.

11

Praying for Someone You Don't Want to Pray For

So Samuel called to the LORD, and the LORD sent thunder and rain that day; and all the people greatly feared the LORD and Samuel. And all the people said to Samuel, "Pray for your servants to the LORD your God, that we may not die; for we have added to all our sins the evil of asking a king for ourselves." Then Samuel said to the people, . . . "The LORD will not forsake His people, for His great name's sake, because it has pleased the LORD to make you His people. Moreover, as for me, far be it from me that I should sin against the LORD in ceasing to pray for you."

1 Samuel 12:18–20, 22–23

Have you ever noticed that there are people in our lives that we stop praying for? I think we have all done this at some time or other. Perhaps we do not like what they are doing or what they have done. We may have little or no interest in the interests they have or the circles they move in; or we may passionately oppose the standards they hold—or do not hold. Their attitudes or actions irritate or inconvenience us, bug us or become painful to us. They become people we "sign off" from, too easily forgetting the heart of God who is as relentlessly committed to sinners now as He was in sending His Son.

That, in fact, is the center-point against which our patience with sinners is to be measured. Hear it again:

> For when we were still without strength, in due time Christ died for the ungodly. For scarcely for a righteous man will one die; yet perhaps for a good man someone would even dare to die. But God demonstrates His own love toward us, in that while we were still sinners, Christ died for us.
>
> Romans 5:6–8

I invite you to candidacy for an anointing of love. The story from God's Word before us reveals and exudes a divine love that even when heartbroken, refuses to be diminished. The text of the story is a perfect example. It unveils God working His love in the heart of a person who had all but spat in His face.

God's heart *is* on the side of *every* human being! This does not mean He endorses everything anyone does. But while it is not an endorsement, His love does demonstrate an *engagement*, and it is our *engaging* those we would rather not pray for that helps us have His heart. How? By welcoming God to fill us with the Holy Spirit of patience and persistence, transforming us to have a heart to reach and a passion to pray.

As we process this together, we may discover the ease with which you or I can absorb the world's disposition toward prejudice, hatefulness or reactionary rejection of others. We may be confronted with the contrast between God's love for the world and ours. But these pages are important, pivotal even, for some who read to become freed from attitudes that have been dominated by our personal or cultural preferences rather than ruled by the Savior who died for us. Ultimately, and demandingly, it starkly asserts to us all

- that whatever righteousness we have gained was unearned, and the actual unrighteousness marking us at the time did not hinder God's will or readiness to accept us "while we were yet sinners." And that . . .
- since, by faith, we have had "the righteousness of God in Christ" conferred upon us, that gift has not authorized us to compare our righteousness with anyone else, nor has it assigned us the task of passing judgment on another, nor has it legitimized negative opinions we have. Rather, it authorizes—and will empower us if we will receive it—a capacity to "love as we have been loved."

Let's turn now to the story. The verses quoted beneath this chapter's title were spoken to the people of Israel by one of their greatest judges during one of their most selfish times in history. That man was the prophet Samuel, and he was a man who understood the heart of God and faithfully lived a devoted life before Him.

If anyone in Scripture characterizes fidelity to God's ways, Samuel is the man. And I want to stress that that fact is solidly backed up by the Scriptures, because we are going to look at him as a case of a person who persisted in prayer until God told him to stop.

The setting for Samuel's birth is about eleven hundred years before Christ. It was a rugged time in Israel's history—the time of the Judges. Spiritual vacillation, ethical and moral instability—all were wildly at risk. Rarely is consistency found here except to sin, and even efforts at doing right turned awry since what was "right" was subject to anyone's interpretation. "Everyone did what was right in his own eyes" (Judges 21:25).

A Prophetic Voice Rises

The early pivot point in 1 Samuel, the first of the pair of Bible books named after him, relates that at this time there was no "open vision." This expression explains the people's loss of spiritual and social perspective. God's prophetic message—the proclamation of His Word—was unknown: No trumpet for truth resounded. But God was getting ready to change that.

The Tabernacle of the Lord was now located in Shiloh, west of the Jordan and about forty miles north of present-day Jerusalem, and that is where the people gathered for special festivals.

We are introduced to Hannah, a dear woman with a loving husband, Elkanah, but with a broken heart: She had no children. And it was one year at the worship festival in Shiloh that she prayed God would remove her barrenness. She pledged, "If You give me a son, Lord, I'll raise him for Your ministry—pledging him to You for Your purpose." During that year, she became pregnant and Samuel was born. His name means "answered prayer."

True to her word, as soon as the child was weaned Hannah and Elkanah presented Samuel to Eli, Israel's high priest, that he might be raised there in the Tabernacle in the service of the Lord. It was after his early years of being trained by Eli that the spirit of prophecy began to give evidence of God's hand upon him. Everyone in Israel recognized that this young man was given by God to bring spiritual leadership to Israel.

Samuel is referred to by students of the Bible as a "bridge person," one who lived during the era of the judges. Leaders of the preceding era, spanning more than 2,300 years, were soldiers, warriors. Kings followed him. The unique trait of Samuel's leadership was that it was entirely exercised by the raw, dynamic power of prayer. As prophet, he spoke the truth and called the people to accountability. As priest, he revealed God's mercy and invited the people to come to Him through the covenant of sacrifice and forgiveness. He lived out the challenge set before every spiritual leader: to teach and live God's Word boldly, while equally modeling and teaching God's mercy and desire to forgive.

The people loved Samuel dearly. There is not a person who shows greater constancy in his purpose than Samuel. When you see that, you begin to understand why it was such a heartbreaking moment for him when the elders of the people cast aside his leadership and said, "Samuel, make us a king." Two important things occurred at this juncture in Israel's history, and it is at this point in the Word we find great examples of key truths about how to respond to things that would stifle your will to pray for people you would otherwise not even want to think about anymore.

The first was the way both Samuel and God responded to the people's demands. Samuel was grief-stricken and overwhelmed by feelings of rejection. God's response was to clarify for Samuel what was really happening. The Lord said to him, "Samuel, don't feel rejected. They are not rejecting you; they are rejecting Me." While this grieved Samuel's heart even more, he followed the Lord's direction to let the people have their king.

But then we see the other important thing. Samuel, understanding the heart of God, was able to enter this fact into the record: Even though the people reject God, God will never reject His people. Look once again at his words: "The LORD will not forsake His people, for His great name's sake, because it has pleased the LORD to make you His people" (1 Samuel 12:22). In other words, God's mercy will never fail.

This is a very important thing to see. They rejected the Lord's rule in their midst, and the Lord allowed them to do it. God never commandeers a human being's destiny. Every person has free choice. God offers His way of design and purpose, but if that is rejected He will not force the issue. *But neither will He forsake His people.* God does not revoke His commitment. He will not love any less those who choose their own way.

God does not sign off on people who sign off on Him.

Coronation Day

On this occasion, when the people affirmed their desire for a king and rejected Samuel as the spokesperson for God's rule as King of Israel, a pair of things occurred.

First, Samuel asked the people to stand and see a "great thing which the LORD will do before your eyes" (verse 16). Then he prayed, asking God to send thunder and rain, and instantly an absolutely earthshaking display from the skies brought sheets of rain upon the assembled multitude. It was God's hand of power, reminding the people of a similar occasion years before, when a great deliverance was brought about because of Samuel's prayer.

On that occasion, a gathered host of troops had been put to wild flight, and Israel's troops pursued them and won the day after Samuel had asked God to show His power on His people's behalf. Their helplessness was turned to victory. They triumphed, notwithstanding limited troop strength and woefully weak weaponry compared to their well-fitted opponents. God's message was unmistakably clear: The God of Israel *is* a mighty God who is able to lead to military victory. Their rejection of Samuel was really a rejection of Him, a choice they were making because they wanted "a king . . . like all the nations" (1 Samuel 8:5). God was fully adequate for their need, as defender as well as provider, if they would have Him. But that would require a walk of faith, and they were opting to walk in the wisdom of the world.

So on this day, as Samuel yielded to their insistent quest for an earthly king, the explosive storm reminded them afresh of God's power when people of faith pray—and they were suddenly stricken with remorse. They cried out to Samuel to pray for them "that we may not die; for we have added to all our sins the evil of asking a king for ourselves" (1 Samuel 12:19).

In response, Samuel turned to them and said, "You have done wickedly, you have done unwisely, but God will not divorce Himself from you. *But far be it from me that I should sin against the Lord in ceasing to pray for you*" (see verses 20–23).

121

How Shall I Think—and How Shall I Pray?

In the news, on stage, in so much music and in the constant stream of newer, more decadent films, we see people parading and promoting ungodly behavior. We resist, we take a stance against the values represented, not because of the people involved, but because the things being advanced are destructive to society's health, which is why God's Word prohibits them. But too often, we mix our distaste for the behavior with irritation and hate for the people: "Those people make me sick!" We are vulnerable to becoming even more disappointed when civil or spiritual leaders waffle on issues of righteousness.

We are prone to turn our backs in disgust at neighbors who are just distasteful—rejecting these citizens-become-my-enemies just as much as they are hating and rejecting people like you and me. We are capable of compromising our discipleship under Jesus' Lordship, not by the values we hold but by the spirit in which we respond to those whose values offend Him. Antagonized, we are tempted to become antagonists, rather than responding like Samuel, who refused to cease caring for and praying for God's opponents. We forget Christ's call to Kingdom lifestyle and attitude: "Love your enemies. Pray for those who despitefully use you and persecute you."

It would be a good thing for us to review God's words periodically: "The rejection is of Me, not you—but I'm not giving up on them." To be renewed in God's Spirit via this truth will enable us to receive the tone and behavior Samuel displayed, and reflect the spirit of his response in our own circumstances: "Far be it from me that I should sin against the Lord in ceasing to pray for you."

122

This reminds me of my need to ask myself this question: Is there anyone I have stopped praying for? I might not even *care* that I stopped—if I even recognize it. I might even *justify my spite* with self-righteous indignation. But to do either is to forget that God, who *alone* has the holy right to reject offending injustice or sin, *never gives up caring*—and my Father calls me to mirror His heart and never give up praying.

Next, if I am willing to pray with a heart of passion for sinners who indulge in the perverse, the shameful and the corrupt and who do it with glee, will my passion be driven by my anger or by my sense of God's broken heart for such warping of one of His own creation, for such satanic bondage in a being He longs to know the beauty of His original purpose?

When Sincerity Turns to Sin

When the Bible says that Samuel would not cease to pray, it underscores the point that to cease to pray for a person because of his bad decisions is sin. In what way is it sin? Are we going to hell because we refuse to pray for someone? No. You and I have been secured on the grounds of whom we pray *to*, not whom we pray *for*. Our salvation is secure. I take remarkable comfort in that. In fact, we can gain strength from the fact that God refines our lives and teaches us His values. It gives our lives quality and substance to stand on His values.

But what about those who want to go their own way? Is it "Tough rocks for them"? I would imagine that we do not get up one day and decide that we are through praying for them. What happens is that our hearts lose touch with God's heart for people.

Look at the fifteenth chapter of this same book of 1 Samuel, verses 10–11. At this point Saul has turned from following God's commandments. "Now the word of the LORD came to Samuel, saying, 'I greatly regret that I have set up Saul as king, for he has turned back from following Me, and has not performed My commandments.'" What would you have said if God had said to you, "I greatly regret that this person has done thus and so and has ceased from following Me"? What would you conclude? Would you write that person off? Would you think God was tired of that person, too?

What did Samuel do?

> Samuel went no more to see Saul until the day of his death. Nevertheless Samuel mourned for Saul, and the LORD regretted that He had made Saul king over Israel. Now the LORD said to Samuel, "How long will you mourn for Saul, seeing I have rejected him from reigning over Israel?"
>
> 15:35–16:1

Samuel mourned over Saul until the Lord finally told him to stop! Was Samuel invested with more patience and mercy than God Himself? Not at all. He understood God's mercy and patience. A man who was the product of prayer—whose very name means "answered prayer"—does not give up on God's heart for people.

Like Samuel, among all of us who know the name of Jesus as Savior, there is not one who is not a product of answered prayer. Not one of us. No one was born into the Kingdom apart from somebody praying for us. We may not even know who it was. Someone was laboring in spiritual travail and by the power of the Holy Spirit birthed that which released the life of Christ to us. You and I were born with the name "answered prayer." So, also like Samuel, we are called to be persons of prayer.

I remember several years ago thinking about a church that I had been actively involved in at one time. Sad times had come and there was hardly any vitality in that church. One day that church was on my mind, and as I prayerfully thought of its crippled condition, the Lord spoke to me. He named the church and said, *It is dead.*

I would later discover that I had missed His point, but at that moment I concluded that God had withdrawn His presence, His hand was removed, the glory had departed and *Ichabod* was written over the door. It was destined to be a spiritual bone pile.

Some time later Anna and I were having dinner with a young man, a former staff member of our church, who came from the same community where this other church was. As we were conversing, he began telling us—knowing that I had formerly been involved in that church—that he was friends with the youth pastor there. With excitement, he told us that a spirit of revival had broken out there—that God was beginning to bring that church back. Obviously, he was excited because anyone who rejoices in God-at-work would be. It was a blessing to a community, and souls were coming to Christ!

As he relayed that information, I was happy of course, but I said to the Lord, *I thought You told me that church was dead.* This stayed on my mind, and later I took it to the Lord in prayer. "Lord, I don't understand. I'm happy about this, but I thought You told me that church was dead."

It was in that moment, the Lord whispered words of loving rebuke to me. He said, *Yes, I did. But you thought I was giving you a piece of information, when, in fact, I was trying to call you to pray for that church's resurrection!*

What a lesson: We can even be a recipient of prophetic insight and by reason of not praying it through, misinterpret the meaning of the Holy Spirit by reason of our presuppositions. Samuel never did this. He, in fact, walked with Israel through the season that the name *Ichabod* (Hebrew for "the glory has departed") came to represent, and kept his eyes on God's mercy.

God's Word adds that Samuel "mourned," an expression that means he continued both to fast and pray for Saul. He was angry with his foolishness, wearied by his boneheaded obstinacy, pained by his carnal habits and sick of his persistence on a path that Saul well understood was a spiritual dead-end street. But as much as he did not "like" Saul, he never ceased praying for him. Now, if you know Saul's end, this raises some questions. Not only did Saul go deeper into his own bondage and selfishness and foolishness, he ended up consulting a witch and finally committing suicide. It followed that the nation suffered a devastating defeat. That certainly does not sound like an answer to prayer.

Loved one, listen closely. The whole issue of Samuel's prayer involves God's action in the bigger picture. When you and I pray for God to touch the heart of someone whom we might otherwise give up on, we are instrumental in a release of divine grace because we refuse to sign off. It may well be the thing that leads to the eventual transformation of society itself.

While Samuel was praying in what appears to be the decadent, downward course of Saul that ended in disaster, something else was going on. God was beginning to move by His Spirit in a young shepherd boy out in the fields of Judah. He was beginning to shape a man who would be raised up as leader to the nation. This future leader would become an instrument to extend the boundaries of God's goodness in the land. He was a man who would lead the people in dimensions of praise and worship to God that they had never known. He was a man who so modeled the heart of God that in a future day, the Messiah of God would be called his Son. God was giving rise to that man—to David— as Samuel was praying. Samuel did not sign off until God released him; therefore, God could work.

Hold On in Prayer!

The call of the Lord is on us. We must not be trapped by the supposition that prayer is futile. When people revolt and rebel against God, when they dabble in evil and conspire with the perverse, here is the lesson Samuel teaches us: *It is a sin to cease praying.*

Some time ago, I was surfing TV channels to catch a little of the news before going to bed, when I paused at an interview with one of America's most powerful men in terms of money and media. It caught my attention because I had known this man to say denigrating things about born-again Christians and the Word of God.

As I listened to the conversation, I was grateful for the compassion I felt in my heart. I have no cause for any degree of self-righteousness about that because that would not always have been true in my life. I can remember watching demonstrations on television that would infuriate me because of the cause being advocated. I can remember times I would feel sick over it—not with illness but with internal anger. I would boil over with indignation, born of self-righteousness I did not even recognize.

But watching this man I felt two things. One, I did not feel superior to him in any wise. If the Bible shows anything, it is there in Samuel's words: God loves this man just as much as He loves me. The fact that he has made particular anti-biblical choices has nothing to do with God's heart and attitude toward him. God cannot work in this man's life the saving grace He would like unless the man will receive it, but that does not change God's heart.

And, two, I felt moved with gratitude. I thought, *Lord, I want to pray for this man.* Something began to move in my heart. I do not know what will happen in his life, but I do know this: Great things might be accomplished if Christians would pray instead of signing off on others whom we dislike, disapprove of or are disgusted or disappointed by.

Suppose your neighbor next door throws an absolutely infuriating party every Saturday night. You wish there were an answer, but you see none short of moving. Now suppose that in the private place of your heart you move aside self-righteousness and judgment and say, "God forbid that I would ever sin against You, Lord, in not praying for this man." And you pray for that neighbor with love—with genuine love. How might God be able to work?

There was a man who had been raised in a town called Tarsus, which is located in modern-day Turkey. He had a brilliant mind and was a strong leader, but he was creating his own private holocaust in the Church. The Church went to prayer, and the power of God encountered Saul of Tarsus on the way to Damascus. In one blinding moment of revelation, this man was changed through an encounter with Jesus Christ, but it took two men to bring him into acceptance with the Church: Ananias, the man who risked being martyred by being available to witness to Saul (see Acts 9), and Barnabas, the leader who found Saul (Paul) when he had been distanced by the fear of the believing community and brought him into ministry (see Acts 9:27). The Body of Christ will correspondingly advance in a fresh spirit of revival when praying people let the Lord open their hearts to people other believers dodge.

Think of this call to pray for those you would tend to reject by making a prayer list—keeping a person on it for at least a week or more to let melt into your heart the Holy Spirit's feeling about him or her. Start praying for God to bless people outside of your comfort zone—and not just the rich and famous folks, though they could use it very much. Pray for that cousin who betrayed you. Pray for the people next door or people at the office, those who irritate and cause rancor. Pray for situations in governments that need godly intervention or special interest groups that represent corrupted moral values. And pray for the gas station attendant, waitress or store clerk who irritated you by lack of service, being smart-faced or being sassy. But in all, when you start to say, "I don't like this pers—" stop mid-sentence and say, "Lord, how do You want me to pray for this person?"

Let's allow our hearts to be dominated by the spirit that characterized Samuel when he said, "Far be it from me that I should sin against the Lord in ceasing to pray for you." Do you have a difficult case to pray for? Let's look in the next chapter at two resources the Lord has given us to help us persevere.

12

HOW TO PRAY
WITHOUT CEASING

Rejoice always, pray without ceasing, in everything give
thanks; for this is the will of God in Christ Jesus for
you.

1 Thessalonians 5:16–18

Thessalonians! The one word takes me back to my childhood. I can remember distinctly that this word signi-
fied my two least favorite books in the Bible, and there
were two reasons. The first reason was that they were so
hard to find when I tried to look them up. The second
was that, for some bizarre reason, the name *Thessalonians*
sounded weird to me—like a strange vegetable. "What are

we having tonight for dinner? *Thessalonians?* Oh, no, not those again!"

The city of Thessalonica still exists today. Salonica it is called; the *Thes* part at the beginning is no longer present in its name these two thousand years later, but people still live and work there.

Why am I telling you this? Because praying for our loved ones involves learning to apply practical "praying without ceasing." And the consummate biblical teaching for accomplishing that comes from these two little books written to everyday people in a city whose story spans ancient days to contemporary Greece, where there are still strong and vibrant congregations present—something to which I can testify because I have been there.

These two epistles, also written by the apostle Paul, have one common theme, and they stand out from the rest of the New Testament as unique in this regard. They focus as no other books in the Bible on the Second Coming of the Lord Jesus Christ. This topic was the heartbeat not only of these letters but also of the life of the Thessalonians themselves. Their hearts resonated passionately with the written messages brought to them about the return of the Lord.

The story of the founding of the church in Thessalonica is a miracle in its own right, not only because many people came to Christ—and that is obviously a miracle—but also because it happened in such a short time. In just a matter of weeks a strong church was established. The Bible makes special note that in Berea, a neighboring community of Thessalonica, the same thing occurred. They, too, were people who, when the Word of God was opened to them, understood that the promised Messiah had come in the Person of Jesus, and they responded immediately. Paul had moved on to other places of ministry but received correspondence from the Thessalonians. He wrote these letters to encourage them.

Throughout each of these epistles, as I mentioned, there is recurrent reference to the return of Jesus. There are more than 280 references to the Second Coming of Jesus Christ in the whole New Testament, and the books of 1 and 2 Thessalonians are large contributors.

However, the command to pray without ceasing stands out as one of a group of terse directives near the end of the first epistle. They are apostolic points for keeping your life on the cutting edge while serving the Lord and anticipating His return in faithful stewardship of the new life and power He has given us. Most of these admonitions—seventeen of them in just twelve verses, verses 11–22 in chapter 5—are challenging but not unreasonable requests. And I want to target verse 17 because it is the theme of that chapter and verse 18 because of the door it opens to confronting the Church's greatest threat to dynamic prayer. Let's begin with the first: "Pray without ceasing."

How can we even begin to fulfill that command? There are a number of ways *not* to fulfill it. I remember as a child hearing—more than once—that believers must pray without ceasing. This was taught to me in some of my earlier years in a way that induced guilt. In fact, it made me feel hopeless. The words were something like, "We're all supposed to pray, but none of us prays enough."

That was all anybody needed to say to make you wince: *Yes*, I would think. *Yes, you're right. I know that.* And then the second punch: "The least we could do is pray an hour a day."

Now I think most people (and I hope God as well) think I am serious about prayer. And I have no question that there are times that we need to reevaluate the *duration of time* we give it. Further, I have no desire to reduce patterns of response God has placed in anyone's heart as to your daily quantity of time, or the time (even days) given at special seasons. But there is something about proposing apparent standards of acceptability, suggesting that "If you're really serious, you certainly won't fall beneath this daily measure."

I think others share my experience along the following lines.

During *early* experiences of trying to cultivate a healthy prayer life, I can remember as a teenager having this happen. The teen-time of life is not the only time we might face this, of course. Does it sound familiar?

After getting on your knees with the intention of praying for a good half hour, you begin: "Oh, Lord! Hallelujah! Here I am today." You start reciting your prayer list and you are sincere and you feel so good, praying so diligently. After a while you think, *Wow, I'm on a roll!* You continue, reciting everything you can think of and saying each three different ways, feeling, *This is happening today. I'm doing it.* Then you look at your watch—and you have been praying for four and a half minutes. You stop, hiding your next thought from God if possible, and think, *I'm out of steam. What do I do now? I've got 25 and a half minutes to go!*

Have you been there? We chuckle about those things, but most of us know the reality of feeling guilt-ridden by the pressure to achieve a time mark. And then somebody says, "But, truly, what the Bible tells us to do is pray without ceasing. How can He answer our prayers for our loved ones if we don't do what He says?" And then discouragement sets in. *This is never going to happen. I mean, Lord, how can I pray without ceasing?*

There have been all kinds of rationales given for this seeming discrepancy, and explanations that might make the directive possible. Here are two reasonable approaches to this challenge.

The First Approach

The essence, of course, is to live in the Spirit of prayer, meaning, in every situation you face—pray.

I think that I have learned a little more about the power of this pray-now-over-everything-you-handle-through-the-day way of life in just the last few years. As years accumulate, the demands on each of us increase. I know the things that I encounter. I know the absolute helplessness I feel when I face the things that are the charge and duty of my life. Theoretically, I have the basic skills, but I learned a long time ago that the skills you have are not really what makes life work. The cutting edge of your life is not based on particular skills and accomplishments you have made or are capable of making. What makes life work is the presence of God upon it all, the Holy Spirit doing something that transcends human ability.

So, initially, that means living in the place of literally launching every issue to the Lord, immediately, "casting all your care upon Him, for He cares for you" (1 Peter 5:7). "Cast your burden on the LORD, and He shall sustain you; He shall never permit the righteous to be moved" (Psalm

55:22). "In all your ways acknowledge Him, and He shall direct your paths" (Proverbs 3:6).

You can live in these promises throughout the day, for example: Suppose you are talking about a matter with someone—maybe someone who has been on your heart for a particular need. If it is someone with whom you can pray, perhaps you could say, "Could we just stop for a moment and ask the Lord about that?"

If it is not someone with whom you can pray because he or she would not understand—that one is not a believer, is not interested, would think that you are some kind of fanatic—then when the conversation is over you can begin breathing your prayer as you move to your next task. If the issue is large, take a brief walk to speak your heart to God. It is not necessary—though it is desirable if possible—to kneel. God can hear you with your eyes closed or open, though it assists focus to close them in most settings. The point is, the posture of prayer is not a prerequisite, but its unceasing practice is powerful. That is living in the Spirit of prayer. That is a life that is moving in a flow of prayer.

For us to develop God's call to prayer in the spirit of joy, we look at the verse "pray without ceasing" first in the light of the preceding verse: "Rejoice always." In other words, while you are praying without ceasing always be rejoicing. And then the ensuing phrase fits in: "In everything give thanks." So in 1 Thessalonians 5:16–18 we see that on each side of this command to pray without ceasing are the words *rejoice always* and *give thanks* in everything. Rejoicing and giving thanks go along with praying without ceasing. Praying for your loved ones will take on a new dimension of freedom as you move into this style of prayer.

The Second Approach

There is another way that has touched my heart in recent days with a profound freshness. How best to pray without ceasing? I can give a one-word response: *Sing*.

The beautiful thing about singing is that praying without ceasing becomes a joy. When you sing, walking in the spirit of prayer is not cumbersome or a burden. There is no limitation, no time constraint, no statistic involved. It releases us from the impossibility of a goal that we tried to reach but wound up woefully short of.

Let's look at some of the reasons we can be encouraged to consider singing as a means of praying without ceasing.

Song Invites God's Presence

The first reason is because song invites God's presence. Psalm 100 tells us that the summons of the Lord is to enter His gates with thanksgiving and enter His courts with praise. Psalm 22:3 says that the Lord is "enthroned in" or inhabits the praises of His people. This verse is quoted often. I suppose there is hardly anyone reading these words who is not familiar with it, and it is a powerful promise.

The truth is, we live in an alienated atmosphere. We have already discussed how our world is poisoned by more than just environmental pollution and human sinning: There is also a prevailing, reigning spirit of darkness. The devil comes to steal, to kill and to destroy. In those three words you have the summary of everything that ruins life. They describe all that deprives, that throttles to death and that ruins in one way or another. You see it in the lives of the people you love; you see it where you work; you see it in your neighborhood.

The Bible says that it is our call as a people to provide a place for the entry of God's rule instead of the present tyrannical rule of hell over souls and circumstance. So in the face of dark or difficult times, sing praise! It is more than just whistling in the dark. You are exalting the Source of all light and invoking His glory to enter your world.

As we look further into the power of song, I want to introduce here some thoughts about "Christian fatalism." As you will see, we are now turning to the command in verse 18, "In everything give thanks," and our discussion here is intended to deal with a demanding and delicate subject. But to address it rightly and wisely in the light of all the Scriptures is to gain another principle, or conviction, that will contribute to helping us obey God's call: "Keep on praying and don't stop for anything!"

Song Counters "Christian Fatalism"

First, let me assert boldly that I do not judge the sequence of commands in verses 17–18 to be random, but very intentional. "In everything give thanks" is obviously possible because song is a means of sustaining prayer through praise. That is simple to establish, but I have encountered significant confusion through the years with what I believe is a sad distortion of the meaning of the rest of the verse. Something of a fatalistic interpretation of verse 18 crops up often, suggesting that "everything," of necessity, would include bad things—things that reduce life, faith and hope. This leads next to the notion that we are to give thanks for these bad things because God says so, whether we like it or not.

I am not countering the idea that we are called to sing and praise God for solely sweet and lovely things, but let me develop this. I have heard thousands of leaders as well as lay individuals say that the following removed a blur from their vision and expanded their faith and boldness in praying for those they lead, those they serve and those they love.

There is no contesting the fact that confronting the terrible or traumatic with triumphant praise is not a casual practice. But even in the darkest personal times of your life, song is an instrument of healing and breakthrough. I remember when my son-in-law Scott Bauer was suddenly taken by the explosive hemorrhaging of a brain aneurism. Our daughter Rebecca was stricken with shock, grief and emotional upheaval, as were her children. The congregation he pastored loved him dearly, and was grieved as well. But it was uplifted in faith when they learned that Rebecca had asked that the following Sunday (and for weeks to come) they would join her in singing "Blessed Be the Name of the Lord" by Matt Redman.

Her response was neither "religious" nor a sign of denial or pretention. It was rooted in the soil of solid understanding that the praise being offered was not required by God as an act of approval for the death of her husband. She knew the distinction between "victim" and "victor" theology, and her mind—even in grief—remained uncluttered by a common tendency today to tolerate Christian fatalism. That fatalistic view will deter people from praying at all, especially when very, very painful things happen. It prompts them to yield to defeat rather than confront the enemy, to cease praying rather than prevail until God's Spirit signals an intercessory assignment has been completed.

Hosts of sincere Christians have been influenced to think that the truly mature spiritual believer is the one who, without even a sign, simply praises God and accommodates himself to any situation that is painful, stress-filled, explosive, damaging or cataclysmic—and who does it with the oft-stated truism, "Well, this just must be the will of God."

In those few words the supposed spirituality is often a surrender to unbiblical passivity. Thereby, a large percentage of believers forfeit their place of privileged authority in Christ by automatically accepting the given circumstance as being "God's will."

For many, it is a cultural presumption. It prevails because so many believers express it as though it were a statement of faith and quote Bible verses that, at first glance, seem to support the idea. The result is that the world around us—itself, already steeped in a lifestyle that presumes little if anything of God's true Person or power—weaves its mistaken convictions into the fabric of the general argument that, at best, God is someone you take a gamble with because you never know what His next whim will be.

Take insurance policies, for example. Many actually word their documents to protect themselves from liability when there are "acts of God." The whole climate of thought runs something like this: God is basically ticked off, and you never know when or where His next tantrum will take place.

"Acts of God" become synonymous with the worst things that can happen. "Hurricane Katrina? Well, God just got sick and tired of the Caribbean and southeast U.S. so He doubled up His fist and let 'em have it."

The attitude of Christian leaders who see disasters rather automatically as God wreaking judgment often yields high visibility quotes that swell with superiority and confirm to society again: "The religious think they're better than we are, and are getting their kicks to see us get booted around by the Almighty."

When this happens, I often think how easy it is to become self-righteous—especially if the spokesperson happens not to live near the flood plain, in the impact area of the earthquake fault line or in line of the brushfire zone—any place that God is currently zapping.

These events have nothing to do with God. He does not operate a workshop where He hammers out 500-year floods, 7.0 earthquakes or fires that sweep hundreds or thousands of acres while destroying homes and killing thousands, including emergency personnel attempting to stave off the horror at hand. In summary, let me simply say: God did not design tornadoes to sweep down and blast buildings into smithereens and people into oblivion.

Christians are confused about this in part because of the words that immediately follow the Bible's call to us to "pray without ceasing." The next phrase reads, "in everything give thanks; *for this is the will of God in Christ Jesus for you*" (1 Thessalonians 5:17–18, emphasis added). Instead of yielding to fatalism, hear the call: "*Keep praying*, even when tough stuff happens," and *do this by invading the difficult with thanksgiving*, because the truth larger than the problem is that God's power can transform any mess when He is invited into it.

I don't know how often I have heard people mistakenly interpret those words, like this: "Whatever happens to you is the will of God, so the smartest and most spiritual thing you can do is give thanks."

It is spoken as if to say (though these thoughts go unspoken): "I mean, hey, who can resist Him? If He decides to lay one on you and your car gets dented in an accident, you are out $1,850 for damages and you are not going to have a car for three weeks while it gets repaired; then you get a loaner that breaks down in the rain. Well, hey—get over it: God says to praise Him. Get happy and He might give you a hand. The whole thing is His will, you know. What's that, one of Ed's kids broke his leg? Hallelujah! God has His reasons. So your daughter is on drugs and stole your credit cards? Praise God! I don't think we'll ever understand this stuff, but this must be His will."

Look again at 1 Thessalonians 5:18. Don't miss the focus of the words: "In everything give thanks; for this is the will of God in Christ Jesus for you." The message is *not*, "Be thankful *for* everything," but "Give thanks *in* everything"! That is what the will of God is for us: to lift up praise to Him with gratitude for *His* nature, which does not plan the evil, the injurious or the painful, but who—*in these things*—is the only One able to address them in love, resolve them in wisdom, provide for them in grace and transform them by His power. *Give thanks in song for that!*

Song Invites Comfort

People who fall into the trap of passivity or philosophizing theology will oft quote another Scripture, misapplying one of the dearest verses in all of the Bible: "And we know that all things work together for good to those who love God, to those who are the called according to His purpose" (Romans 8:28).

Again, let's pass over the ready idea of supposing "all things" are ordained for good, irrespective of how painful, horrible or miserable. Three things are essential to "get it," when this wonderful verse is quoted:

First, the "things" are what are "good," but it is God's "working them together" that can achieve the interweaving, overlapping and penetrating of the crisis or impossibility with His overarching grace, overwhelming love and overcoming power.

Second, God's intervention is not intended to be singlehanded. He *is* the only One with the necessary power and perfect wisdom, but we are the "ones called" by His purpose to partner with Him in meeting the crisis. That partnership is clearly stated: Our part is to *pray.* Pray?

Yes, because third, the *whole* of the truth is not contained in verse 28. Romans 8:28 is preceded by verses 26–27. This trio of verses *must* become linked in our understanding and in our passion. Listen:

> Likewise the Spirit also helps in our weaknesses. For we do not know what we should pray for as we ought, but the Spirit Himself makes intercession for us with groanings which cannot be uttered. Now He who searches the hearts knows what the mind of the Spirit is, because He makes intercession for the saints according to the will of God.
>
> Romans 8:26–27

Let's let our hearts and minds be tuned to and enlightened by God's Word. The Bible does not say that "everything that happens to us or to others in our world is something that He designed as an expression of His sovereign will. It says that *in those things, through them and beyond them,* He can work

143

an outcome that will be "for the good," but it is *because, if invited, He will step into them*! We must resist the impulse to resign ourselves to difficult or disastrous situations, presuming that because God is sovereign in His power, everything that happens is a preordained part of His sovereign will. Otherwise we wind up attempting to either muddle our way through or accept a religiously conceived philosophy positing that, "Since God is all-powerful and all-wise, if this wasn't what He wanted it wouldn't have happened."

But wait a minute: There will be many who will be lost eternally, and God's Word pointedly says that fact is *never* His will (see 1 Timothy 2:4). So something is awry in any theology that removes prayer from being a God-ordained instrument, in partnership with His power, to release His will into lives and circumstances that are alien to His will.

So when bad things happen, what *is* His will? The answer is in the completed text—all three verses quoted above. Together they justify the opinion that here, in Romans 8, is one of the most comforting truths in God's Word—but it requires responding to the role of Holy Spirit energized, enlightened and empowered prayer. So let's unite the two passages we have studied, from the Thessalonian and the Roman epistles. When bad things happen

- The Spirit helps us in our weaknesses by making intercession. We do not know how to pray, but the Holy Spirit helps our inabilities, giving rise to expressions unutterable apart from His rising within us to pray on target!

What to do? Invite the Spirit of God to fill, overflow and enable you to pray and sing beyond yourself. Quite frankly, that is essentially what the language of the Spirit was given to the Church for at its birth as recorded in Acts 2. We recognize also the potential of the Holy Spirit to reveal insights beyond our own understanding and to enable our praying as well in our natural language, penetrating dark realms with shafts of fire, breaking down strongholds of darkness and drawing souls to the Savior.

- Give thanks, for this is the will of God concerning you.

The spirit of thanksgiving "in everything" (including things that we would ordinarily be slow to be thankful for) is a signal flag, teaching us that praise and thanksgiving are more than declarations of exaltation and gratitude. Both are dynamic means of invading any situation with the spirit that will set in motion the reversal of all that is opposed to God's rule and will, and will remove the capacity of dark powers to reside as "occupying forces" of the adversary. Both also are nurturing to the human spirit—bringing strength and awakening exhilaration in the human soul—bringing refreshing.

My own life and ministry was released immeasurably and much of what has happened in the last forty years is attributable to my learning the power of song—of singing privately each day, and also publicly, and also "with the spirit and with the understanding" (see 1 Corinthians 14:15). It is the easiest, most fulfilling, simplest and most effective means for giving thanks, and is also often the Spirit's way to extend comfort. [See my material on the life-begetting power of song in my books *Worship His Majesty* (Gospel Light, 2000) and *The Reward of Worship* (Chosen, 2007).]

Song Defeats the Enemy

I will just relay briefly a few more points about the efficacy of song. The story in 2 Chronicles 20 gives the incredible account of Jehoshaphat, king of Judah, under attack from neighboring nations and vastly outnumbered by superior hosts. Pursuant upon a prophet's proclamation, "You will not need to fight in this battle, for the battle is the Lord's" (see verse 17), Israel's choir leads the host into battle, the enemy is confounded and its troops turn on themselves.

Song Advances Deliverance

Psalm 32:7 says, "Thou shalt compass me about with songs of deliverance" (KJV). Singing unto the Lord is revealed as a means of constructing a protective wall of God's presence and power, fashioned around you through song. I have spent an hour or more singing in the sanctuary most Saturdays of my pastoral life, usually alone or with a pastoral staff member or two. Among the reasons is the fact that I see this as building a "delivery room" where souls will be delivered into new life in the following day's worship and discipling services.

Song Sustains Spirit Fullness

Ephesians 5:18 commands us to keep on being filled with the Holy Spirit. The tense of the verb makes it clear that spiritual energy needs ongoing renewal. Then it tells us how: by "psalms and hymns and spiritual songs, singing and making melody in your heart to the Lord, giving thanks always for all things to God the Father in the name of our Lord Jesus Christ" (verses 19–20).

Keep singing. As you sing you make a place for the ongoing display of God's working and power. This is not solely a group matter, and it certainly does not have to do with the quality of your voice. God says sing: He likes the way you sound!

The Bible gives us a call to pray without ceasing. Let us apply these principles to ourselves. Let us walk in the wisdom of the truth and pray about everything. Let it be with the spirit of song. Let us sing about God's great glory. Let us praise Him. Let us sing our way into tomorrow.

13

Framing
a Family Picture

It shall be a statute forever.

Exodus 28:43

As I was completing this book, Anna and I celebrated Thanksgiving with almost all our family. The two of us, married now for over fifty years, have become something of a crowd. With us and our four children, Rebecca, Jack, Mark and Christa; their spouses and their children (we have eleven grandchildren); and our grandkids' spouses and their children—which gives us a beginning handful of great-grandchildren—the whole lot now numbers 32! Not only was it a wonderful day, with our kids coming from Wisconsin, Colorado and Canada to be with those of us living in Southern California, but it was highlighted by a time of taking family pictures—of each family, with Anna and me, and with the whole family in one big pic!

Family pictures are a joy to experience and to study. Each face holds innumerable memories—and each person holds great significance for this life and eternal fulfillment in the next by God's purpose for each one. This book has focused on how that purpose, with its significance and fulfillment for each of those you love, may be recovered, realized and secured in Christ—and the role your prayers play in seeing that brought about. I have not written about lighting candles or about making substitute repentance or baptism for family members; no ritual or proxy plans are described in God's Word—but prayer is! It is as clearly taught as it is wonderfully underwritten by God's promise, and it will be enabled by the power of His Spirit.

Take Your Stand

In God's Word there is a beautiful statement that puts the family and life's primary relationships together with the reality of spiritual warfare and the promise of victory. Ephesians 5:21–6:18 addresses the full scope of family relationships and the invisible-but-real fight against the adversary's assault on all God's best for people, their homes, their businesses and their well-being.

First, note the clear and direct way this passage joins those we love with that orderly prayer life to which we're called in partnership with God's will and promise—to engage in spiritual warfare against the enemy, who is against all God wants to do in the lives of those for whom we pray. Second, let me highlight a phrase that assures us of eventual victory—words I want to leave with you as we conclude our study in this book: "And having done all, to stand." There is a beauty in the outcome these words declare, paraphrased as, "Stand firm in your prayer partnership with God, and when the smoke and dust of battle have subsided, you'll still be standing—victorious!"

An overview of this concluding portion of Ephesians 5:21–6:18 is worth regular review as you give yourself to praying for those you love.

> Therefore take up the whole armor of God, that you may be able to withstand in the evil day, and having done all, to stand.
>
> Stand therefore, having girded your waist with truth, having put on the breastplate of righteousness, and having shod your feet with the preparation of the gospel of peace; above all, taking the shield of faith with which you will be able to quench all the fiery darts of the wicked one. And take the helmet of salvation, and the sword of the Spirit, which is the word of God; praying always with all prayer and supplication in the Spirit, being watchful to this end with all perseverance and supplication.
>
> Ephesians 6:13–18

These clear directions given to us for "standing" summarize choices we make—practical steps that will gird our whole being with divine resources, guarding us against doubt, discouragement and defeat. With this preparation of our soul (the mind and emotions—that is, our thoughts and feelings), we are to continue "praying always . . . in the Spirit" (by the Holy Spirit's aid and power).

How to continue "praying always" is not a call to redundancy (mere repetition) but to constancy—that is, to a steadfast stance. And as these last pages are left with you, I want to tell you a story from the Hayford family.

The Believer's Priestly Prayer Privilege

It began on a morning years ago when my father came to the breakfast table. Daddy (as I called him throughout my life) had just finished reading from Exodus 28, where the Lord gave directions concerning the garments to be worn by the Old Testament priests when they came before the Lord in worship and prayer. Because the New Testament teaches that every believer in Christ is now given a royal calling as priests unto God through the Savior, Daddy was impressed with the practical implications for us today in light of the directions God gave the priests then.

Having recounted with my Mamma what he had read in Exodus, he said to her, "You know, honey, the Bible tells us that we are called to a priesthood in prayer—a priesthood that is not an ecclesiastical office but a practical, daily privilege." He quoted 1 Peter 2:5: "You also, as living stones, are being built up a spiritual house, a holy priesthood, to offer up spiritual sacrifices acceptable to God through Jesus Christ."

That text sets forth the assignment of Aaron, the first high priest of Israel, and his intercessory role. His clothing for that role involved the preparation of the breastplate and the ephod (a kind of vest with a cluster of large jewels on the front), which had two shoulder straps. Each strap held an onyx stone engraved with the names of six of the tribes of

Israel—twelve total (see Exodus 28:12). This repeated the engraving of the names of each tribe—one on each of the twelve jewels—on the front of the breastplate.

Having reviewed that, Daddy continued, noting verse 29: "So Aaron shall bear the names of the sons of Israel on the breastplate . . . over his heart, when he goes [before the Lord] . . . as a memorial before the Lord continually." Daddy went on to say, "I am very moved by that. The simple fact that God regarded the mere bearing of those names before Him as a priestly action stirred a thought I want us to apply in our prayer for our families." He proceeded to suggest that every day he and my mother begin joining together simply to bring before the Lord their family names (that is, Hayford and Farnsworth, my mother's maiden name).

For example, Daddy said, "Each day at breakfast, let's pray together and say, 'Lord, we ask that You would, by Your Spirit, move in Your grace upon everyone who bears the surname Hayford and everyone who bears the surname Farnsworth. We ask that, by Your Spirit and for Your glory, You would move upon people who bear our family name. Strengthen all who already know Your name, and draw those who do not know You to hear Your Word and receive Your Son.'" They asked other things as well, praying specifically for immediate family members and any issues of which they were aware, but they also began adding that special prayer every day.

It would take far too long to begin reciting the things that began to happen over the next two and a half years as my mother and father added that simple prayer principle to their prayer life together. They experienced some remarkably uncanny results that amazed them, such as obvious cases of divine intervention with individuals of our surname—

people they had never met but who, by divine providence, were brought in touch with them. And to this day, decades later, those I have taught this principle find equally amazing answers occurring as they have begun applying it based on God's Word. With my family, as well as with others, there have been repeated instances of spiritual breakthrough, salvation and personal renewal—and all by simply and continually holding the family name before God in prayer.

These people not only found open doors for witnessing but discovered family members who had received Christ. With surprising regularity, they found that those they "discovered" had only come to Christ since the previously unknown family member began bearing the family name before the Lord.

This is not a testimony reported or a truth related simply as a point of passing interest. As I've said, God's promises are ours to partner with—and in the case of our priestly privileges in Christ, there is even more than we have time or space to relate here. But I want to leave you with two concluding statements:

- God loves you and He loves your family. He has drawn you to Himself and to this book to equip you with understanding and with the spiritual currency in Christ to do business in a prayer partnership with Him.
- Everything of His promise is practical, including your role described in this chapter as a member of God's present priesthood. Nothing of His truth or way is mystical, cultish or religious. Jesus Christ our Lord, by His saving grace and His Spirit's presence in your life, has both qualified you and called you to take your position as a continual bearer of your family before God's throne.

So, dear one, take your stand!

Take your position for the inheritance God wills for your family. Refuse to permit the Intruder to retouch or reduce the beauty of the picture God has for them. He has it in focus and has called you and me to see that everyone is prayed into the picture. Always remember this: Not only are you in it, but as you keep praying for those you love, it will fulfill the pivotal role Father God has given you to see that your final family picture has a bigger frame. He wants every one of them in the picture!

Afterword

Having Done All, Stand

I exhort first of all [that makes it the priority] that supplications, prayers, intercessions, and giving of thanks be
made for all.

1 Timothy 2:1

There are many reasons those we love are resistant to
meeting God. They may not know how. They may be
belligerent. They may not even believe He exists. Our role,
as we have seen, is to love them and then pray the Kingdom
into their lives as we seek the Lord. We come and stand
before God on behalf of those who really do not know how
or are unwilling to come to God on their own.

This is true intercession—bearing people before the Lord
on our shoulders. That call is so clear, and the authority is

given us in Jesus' name. We come then as priests and saints who have been washed in the blood of Christ. Our own unholiness and inadequacy are neutralized because we are justified in Jesus.

The book of Revelation gives us a dramatic picture of this relationship. If any disservice has been done to the Body of Christ, it is that relegating of the book of Revelation, almost in its entirety, to a future date. Almost every scholar I know acknowledges the first three chapters as relevant to the present, but there are many who turn a corner at chapter four and view the rest of the book as prophetic events that will follow the Rapture. That is not a careful consideration of the richness of this book. I want to invite you to see with me a combination of things that are pertinent as we move forward in intercession for those we love.

First, in Revelation 5:1 we are told that Jesus has a scroll in His hand. Why is this significant? In the Garden of Eden, mankind was given charge of the planet. By betraying that trust not only did man fall into sin, but he forfeited dominion of the planet to the adversary. At that point the title deed shifted from Jesus' throne's rule. This passage of Scripture shows us that the title deed to this planet has been returned to the living God.

Second, we are engaged in an age-long struggle that continues to manifest glimpses of that future glory when the King shall come and establish His global reign, ultimately and consummately. In the meantime, Revelation 5:10 says He has cleansed the redeemed for the purpose of serving as priests and kings to our God.

These are ministries that are accomplished through prayer, spiritual warfare, our witness and our proclamation of the

Word of God. It is always in the atmosphere of love that these ministries are to be carried on. Even the warfare is done not with fisticuffs; there is no place for verbal tongue-lashing of those who are lost. Rather we prepare our hearts before God and move in authority in a realm given us in the name of our Lord Jesus Christ.

Revelation 5:8 says that there are golden bowls of incense around the throne of God, and that they contain the prayers of the saints. There is actually quite a bit in the Bible about bowls. Long ago, for instance, God said to Abraham that judgment had not yet come upon the Amorites because the cup of indignation was not yet full. This tells us that sin has a way of accumulating its force until finally it overflows and judgment comes—not because God is ticked off and comes slinging vengeance at mankind like mud, but because the accumulation of people's own sinning fills the cup to over-flowing and brings inevitable retaliation in the cosmic order of things. God judges not because He delights to do so, but because there comes a time when He says injustice can no longer prevail. Something has to be done.

That something is prayer.

The Bible reveals that there is a cup of intercession as well as a cup of indignation. The power of the prayers of the saints has a way of counterbalancing imminent judgment. When God's people move into prayer (Ezekiel 22:30 uses the phrase "stand in the gap"), God holds off divine judgment until another season. Not only does He reserve judgment, He also executes mercy. Why does this happen? Because the bowls of sin in the scales of justice have been balanced by bowls that are filled to overflowing with the prayers of saints.

Mark 1:15 records these words of Jesus: "The time is fulfilled, and the kingdom of God is at hand." In saying this, I believe that Jesus was talking about a moment to be seized. His words certainly had to do with the introduction of His ministry, but there is another meaning as well. Everything about Jesus' ministry that is "this moment" in its Kingdom manifestation of grace is in a timeless continuum because "Jesus Christ is the same yesterday, today, and forever" (Hebrews 13:8).

There comes, then, in the divine order of things, moments when one of two things will happen. Either the sufficiency of prayers poured toward heaven will invite the rule of God into human affairs and thereby welcome a divine display of grace, or the bowl of evil will fill to overflowing, and judgment will come.

Let your prayers for your loved ones rise to the throne. This is the moment to be seized. Ultimately the King of glory will come and establish His global reign. In the meantime, God is standing in the wings, ready to guide us in praying for those we love.

The book of Hebrews gives us further invitation: "Let us . . . come boldly to the throne of grace, that we may obtain mercy and find grace to help in time of need" (4:16). Do you need His help in bringing your loved ones before the throne? Then He says, "Come boldly and you will receive all the help you need."

Will you join me? Let's move forward in confidence.

Appendix A

A Prayer for Receiving Christ as Lord and Savior

It seems possible that some earnest inquirer may have read this book and somehow still never have received Jesus Christ as personal Savior. If that is true of you—that you have never personally welcomed the Lord Jesus into your heart to be your Savior and to lead you in the matters of your life—I would like to encourage you and help you to do that.

There is no need to delay, for an honest heart can approach the loving Father God at any time. So I would like to invite you to come with me, and let's pray to Him right now.

If it is possible there where you are, bow your head, or even kneel if you can. In either case, let me pray a simple prayer first and then I have added words for you to pray yourself.

My Prayer

Father God, I have the privilege of joining with this child of Yours who is reading this book right now. I want to thank You for the openness of heart being shown toward You and I want to praise You for Your promise, that when we call to You, You will answer.

I know that genuine sincerity is present in this heart, which is ready to speak this prayer, and so we come to You in the name and through the cross of Your Son, the Lord Jesus. Thank You for hearing.[1]

And now, speak your prayer.

Your Prayer

Dear God, I am doing this because I believe in Your love for me, and I want to ask You to come to me as I come to You. Please help me now.

First, I thank You for sending Your Son, Jesus, to earth to live and to die for me on the cross. I thank You for the gift of forgiveness of sin that You offer me now, and I pray for that forgiveness.

Forgive me and cleanse my life in Your sight, through the blood of Jesus Christ. I am sorry for anything and everything I have ever done that is unworthy in Your sight. Please take away all guilt and shame, as I accept the fact that Jesus died to pay for all my sins and that through Him I am now given forgiveness on this earth and eternal life in heaven.

1. Jack Hayford, *I'll Hold You in Heaven* (Ventura, Calif.: Regal, 2003), 38–39. Used by permission.

I ask You, Lord Jesus, please come into my life now. Because You rose from the dead, I know You are alive and I want You to live with me—now and forever.

I am turning my life over to You and from my way to Yours. I invite Your Holy Spirit to fill me and lead me forward in a life that will please the heavenly Father.

Thank You for hearing me. From this day forward, I commit myself to Jesus Christ, the Son of God. In His name, Amen.[2]

2. Ibid., 39–40.

Appendix B

A Prayer for Inviting the Lord to Fill You with the Holy Spirit

If you would like to invite the Lord to fill you with the Holy Spirit, here is a prayer you may wish to use. I am not asking you to say "Amen" at the end of this prayer, because after inviting Jesus to fill you, it is good to begin to praise Him in faith. Praise and worship Jesus, simply allowing the Holy Spirit to help you do so. He will manifest Himself in a Christ-glorifying way, and you can ask Him to enrich this moment by causing you to know the presence and power of the Lord Jesus. Don't hesitate to expect the same things in your experience as occurred to people in the Bible. The spirit of praise is an appropriate way to express that expectation; and to make Jesus your focus, worship as you praise. Glorify Him and leave the rest to the Holy Spirit.

Dear Lord Jesus, I thank You and praise You for Your great love and faithfulness to me. My heart is filled with joy whenever I think of the great gift of salvation You have so freely given to me. And I humbly glorify You, Lord Jesus, for You have forgiven me all my sins and brought me to the Father.

Now I come in obedience to Your call.

I want to receive the fullness of the Holy Spirit. I do not come because I am worthy myself, but because You have invited me to come. Because You have washed me from my sins, I thank You that You have made the vessel of my life a worthy one to be filled with the Holy Spirit of God.

I want to be overflowed with Your life, Your love and Your power, Lord Jesus. I want to show forth Your grace, Your words, Your goodness and Your gifts to everyone I can.

And so with simple, childlike faith, I ask You, Lord, to fill me with the Holy Spirit. I open all of myself to You to receive all of Yourself in me.

I love You, Lord, and I lift my voice in praise to You. I welcome Your might and Your miracles to be manifested in me for Your glory and unto Your praise.

About Jack Hayford Ministries

"Reaching to Touch, Teaching to Change"

Jack Hayford Ministries (also known as Living Way Ministries) is a nonprofit outreach dedicated to strengthening the Body of Christ through the teaching ministry of Pastor Jack Hayford, founding pastor of The Church On The Way in Van Nuys, California (1969–99). Dr. Hayford is also founder and chancellor of The King's College and Seminary in Los Angeles.

The Ministry

Pastor Jack Hayford is known for his practical approach to the Word of God, with an emphasis on growing in Spirit fullness. His weekly television program, *Spirit Formed*, and his daily *Living Way* radio program are broadcast worldwide and via the Web. The ministry's online bookstore distributes the extensive catalog of his audio, video and published resources. For local TV and radio station listings, or to watch, listen or order resources, visit www.jackhayford .org, where you will also find a daily devotional and free resource downloads.

The King's College and Seminary

The King's College and Seminary is an accredited Spirit-filled training center designed to equip men and women for effective, godly leadership in the Church and the community. To learn more about programs of study, call 1-888-779-8040 or visit the websites below.

The King's College (www.kingscollege.edu) is a Spirit-filled, interdenominational postsecondary institution dedicated to preparing men and women who are pursuing God's greatest fruitfulness for their lives. Students can complete their entire degree online without leaving their home or current work and ministry.

The King's Seminary (www.kingsseminary.edu) is a professional graduate school offering ministry training to Spirit-filled men and women, and is the only accredited Pentecostal/Charismatic seminary on the West Coast of North America. Students can complete their program through a combination of online and three-day modular courses at our campus in Los Angeles, California.

The Hayford Bible Institute (www.kingscollege.edu), located on the campus of The King's College and Seminary, is committed to equipping believers to be effective, Spirit-filled instruments of Jesus Christ in an inviting, noncredit environment.

The Jack W. Hayford School of Pastoral Nurture (www.jack hayford.org) is a leadership advancement program that reaches scores of pastors from multiple denominations. It is focused on ministry effectiveness, personal growth and renewal. Consultations are held in a small-group setting in which 45 pastors spend time interacting with Jack Hayford. Nationally acknowledged as a "pastor to pastors," Pastor Jack shares insights gained during his more than fifty years in ministry.

The Online School of Pastoral Nurture (OSPN) (www.jack hayford.org) provides ministry and spiritual enrichment resource materials for pastors, Sunday School teachers, small group leaders and personal study. OSPN subscribers have unlimited access to a growing library of sermon summaries/ outlines from the ministry of Jack Hayford, as well as articles, book excerpts and an online prayer circle. Visit the OSPN sample pages at www.jackhayford.org.

RELATED RESOURCES
BY JACK HAYFORD

Available at www.jackhayford.org
or by calling toll-free 1-800-776-8180
(outside the U.S., call 1-818-779-5593)

Family and Prayer

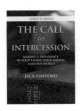

The Call to Intercession

Gain a clear understanding of the intercessory role of the Church, the call and challenges of being an intercessor and how to effectively pray and intercede for your family. Three messages from the *Spirit Formed* TV broadcast on DVD. Also on CD or cassette.

Fixing Family Fractures

Learn how broken relationships can be mended by the power of God and the principles of His Word. Four-message album on CD or cassette.

Blessing Your Children

Discover the importance of encouraging, blessing and correcting the children in your life, and how to leave them a spiritual inheritance. Hardcover book or DVD.

As for Me and My House

Pastor Jack's mother, Dolores Hayford (1916–97), shares a fun, practical plan for effective family devotions. Paperback book.

Your Financial Liberation

Learn the process Pastor Jack and his wife, Anna, went through as a young couple to learn God's principles of stewardship and giving. Three-message album on CD or cassette.

Growing in Christ

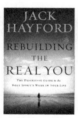

Rebuilding the Real You

Jack Hayford's landmark teaching on the book of Nehemiah unfolds a clear picture of the nature and work of the Holy Spirit, assisting the believer in rebuilding life's broken places. Paperback book.

Living the Spirit-Formed Life

Discover victorious living in Christ through spiritual disciplines such as prayer and fasting, daily worship and the release of repentance and forgiveness. Paperback book or DVD.

Hayford Sexual Integrity Series

This three-book series (*Fatal Attractions, The Anatomy of Seduction, Sex and the Single Soul*) offers compassionate, biblical guidance for believers. Paperback.

Newborn

Pastor Jack's "welcome to the family" outlines basic elements for new believers beginning their life with Christ. Paperback book.

Believers Basics

The key practices essential for growth are worship, fellowship, submission, intercession, witnessing and stewardship. Six-message album on CD or cassette.

Encouragement and Faith

Hope for a Hopeless Day

The seven things Jesus said on the cross provide us with a model for those days in which everything in our world seems to be without hope. Paperback book.

The Bridges of God

When you're open to God's promise, when you're puzzled by God's pathway and when the enemy is breathing down your neck—you're in line for a miracle! Three-message album on CD or cassette.

I'll Hold You in Heaven

This bestselling classic ministers sensitive answers to troubling questions for parents who have lost a child due to miscarriage, SIDS or abortion. Paperback book.

An Unshakable Kingdom

When God's Kingdom penetrates our lives, we may be shocked by circumstances, but we will not be shaken by them. Two-message album on CD or cassette.

Seeing the Heart of God

Only God, through His mercy, forgiveness and desire for our fulfillment, can provide us with the genuine love and acceptance we need. Five-message album on CD or cassette.